CW01018862

WEDLOCKED?

Family Life Series

Edited by Martin Richards, Ann Oakley, Christina Hardyment and the late Jacqueline Burgoyne.

Published

David Clark and Douglas Haldane, *Wedlocked?*
Janet Finch, *Family Obligations and Social Change*
Lydia Morris, *The Workings of the Household*
Philip Pacey, *Family Art*

Forthcoming

Miriam David, *Mum's the Word: Relations between Families and Schools*
Jean La Fontaine, *Child Sexual Abuse*
Ann Phoenix, *Young Mothers*

Wedlocked?

Intervention and Research in Marriage

David Clark and Douglas Haldane

Polity Press

Copyright © David Clark and Douglas Haldane 1990

First published 1990 by Polity Press in association with Basil Blackwell

Editorial office:
Polity Press, 65 Bridge Street,
Cambridge CB2 1UR, UK

Marketing and production:
Basil Blackwell Ltd
108 Cowley Road, Oxford OX4 1JF, UK

Basil Blackwell Inc.
3 Cambridge Center
Cambridge, Massachusetts 02142, USA

ISBN 0 7456 0310 6
ISBN 0 7456 0311 4 (pbk)

British Library Cataloguing in Publication Data
A CIP catalogue record for this book is available from the British Library.

Library of Congress Cataloguing in Publication Data
A CIP catalogue record for this book is available from the Library of Congress.

Typeset in 10 on 12 pt Palatino by Wearside Tradespools, Fulwell, Sunderland
Printed in Great Britain by TJ Press, Padstow, Cornwall

Contents

1

Approaching the Problem

The subject of marriage rarely fails to generate public interest. As an institution undergoing change, or as a relationship offering rewards and penalties, marriage has the capacity to capture the popular imagination. Around 90 per cent of us can expect to be married at some point in our lives; but something like one marriage in three now taking place will end in divorce. A casual observer might therefore easily assume that a great deal is known about marriage and 'marital problems' and that appropriate services have been developed to offer help to those who encounter difficulties in their marriage relationships. Such an assumption is understandable, but false; and much of this book is about the consequences. What we have to say should be of interest to a wide range of individuals, concerned either personally or professionally with understanding marriage and responding to problems within it. Much of our experience in writing the book has been about raising, rather than resolving, a broad spectrum of dilemmas, difficulties and paradoxes. Our intention is to promote further questioning and debate, especially between researchers and practitioners in the field of marriage, who have hitherto led rather separate lives.

Three themes preoccupy us throughout: research into marriage; intervention in marriage; and the development of organizations for undertaking these. There has been far too little communication between social researchers interested in marriage and practitioners conducting marital work. In our view, the development of theory and method in marriage research, and in counselling and therapy has suffered as a result. Only recently have there been some encouraging signs of mutual interest and a willingness to engage with issues and problems held in common. So difficulties in exploring the relationships between research and intervention, are in part a reflection of the current state of the professions. We are unaware of any other works on marriage which have resulted from collaboration between a sociologist and a psychotherapist; our argument might therefore be seen as a test for the possibilities of joint work. What we have to say however is by no means limited to the technical aspects of research and intervention; a great deal of the book is taken up with issues to do with the development of services, and in particular with the work of the voluntary marital agencies. We are interested in the mechanisms by which women and men are selected, trained and supported in their work as counsellors and therapists. Although there are regrettably few examples, our paradigm for development is in organizations which simultaneously undertake work in research, intervention *and* training.

Sociologists and medical practitioners have a history of uneasy relationships, so in joining together to write a book about marriage we were conscious from the start of the difficulties we might have to overcome. Our subject matter is well known to produce attitudes and feelings which are deeply divided. In recent years marriage and the problems which surround it have become the battleground for numerous ideological and personal debates. It is not our intention to add to these. Professionally we each have a special interest, though from different theoretical and practical perspectives, in the social and public context in which people live their lives, as well as in the private arena of relationships, the inner world of persons and the structural and dynamic links between them. One of us is primarily a researcher, the other a clinician; however we are both greatly interested and involved in organizations, in the delivery of services, in teaching and training and in the application of research to practice. Although our common focus in the book is around questions of marriage, we came to this shared interest by very different professional routes.

Douglas Haldane graduated from medical school in July 1948, the month when the National Health Service came into being. During general psychiatric training, he developed a special interest in the problems posed by spouses and families of patients and how best to involve them in the treatment of what would now be called the 'index patient'. This interest was later to be developed in the formation of a department of child and family psychiatry (the first in the United Kingdom to carry that name) where increasingly the focus of assessment and treatment, in clinic, domestic setting or residential unit, was on the family as a whole. One result of this work was an appreciation of how frequently the marital problems of parents preceded or were associated with difficulties expressed by their children. This led to the organization within the department of a marital therapy clinic. Later, within the clinical commitments of a university appointment, it was possible to organize a clinic for the assessment and treatment of couples and families. This kind of psychotherapeutic work, together with an interest in the dynamics of groups and organizations, represents a relatively small, though steadily developing proportion of what is available within the psychiatric services of the National Health Service. The conceptual frameworks or models on which it is based, along with the kind of practices it leads to and the forms of service delivery which it may take, are discussed in more detail in later parts of this book.

By contrast, David Clark came to an interest in marital research via postgraduate study in the sociology of religion. A concern with formal and informal systems of belief flowed easily into the development of questions about the meaning of marriage and personal relationships. Initial research in the period 1977–9 into the sociological aspects of divorce, remarriage and stepfamilies progressed into a number of studies: of public attitudes to marriage and family life; of divorce, remarriage and fertility; and of the relationships between employment and marriage. Some of this work was conducted in collaboration with doctors, and grew out of their clinical concerns: for example, problems associated with offering sterilization to women and men who later divorced, remarried and wished to have the operation reversed; or issues concerning the prevalence of what came to be labelled 'the intermittent husband syndrome' among women married to offshore oil workers. Out of this came a growing interest in counselling and in particular a number of contributions to conferences and seminars organized by the then National Marriage Guidance Council, which following the report of an interdepartmental working party, *Marriage Matters*, in 1979, placed a growing emphasis upon linking issues of research and practice in relation to marriage and marital problems.

So a generation apart in age and with very different intellectual and professional roots, we nevertheless come together with a number of shared concerns. We are also both married, each of us to our first spouse, and each of us has three children; the children of one now being parents themselves. We are aware that two married men writing about marriage might present a perspective which is both limited and biased, particularly in relation to gender issues. We can only hope that this is not so. Each of us has benefited from collaborative work on some of the issues raised in this book, with two female colleagues – Una McCluskey and the late Jacqueline

Burgoyne, and the results of that work have been published. Inevitably, our professional views about marriage are affected by our personal histories and experience; whether adversely or beneficially in terms of what we have to say in this book, is for others to judge.

1.1 Developing a Joint Perspective

We are seeking here to create the conditions in which those concerned to be helpful to couples distressed in their marital relationships, or those who as researchers explore the sources and nature of that distress, can examine some of the current debates and conflicts about marriage and marital relationships, find some common ground and consider how best to apply the results. While the book is about research and intervention, it is not a formal review of research, nor a handbook about how to work with couples. We explore possible developments in practice, research and the organization of services, but we have not set ourselves the task of formulating any kind of plan of action. The book does not seek to be objective, in the sense of 'even-handed', giving due weight to a number of points of view and leaving readers to choose what they might find most suitable and appropriate to their circumstances or style. Nor is it only about considering research which can readily be applied to practice, or which grows from the dilemmas and problems of practice, important though such considerations are. Rather it represents an attempt to find and express a language common both to research and practice, which will consider marriage and 'marital problems' in their context of historical and generational change.

We had already shared some thinking about these issues in the early 1980s when in research and teaching appointments, but we came to a more active collaboration during 1984–6 when we were together chairman and director of a marital agency, the Scottish Marriage Guidance Council. Many of the ideas in this book have been influenced by our experiences from that time; thinking, planning, working together and with others on the development of appropriate services for persons distressed in their most intimate couple relationships. To some extent the book is the product of those difficulties and rewards; the successes and failures; the frustrations and hopes; the well-organized ideas and the emotionally primitive conflicts which characterized the work of the organization as it struggled with these issues. Our task, which had components of administration and management, organizational development and delivery of service, focused in particular upon counselling, training and research, and revealed significant common ground in our approaches, stimulating us to consider how best these might be developed. From that shared experience we now hope to create a climate for consultation (a concept about which we shall have much more to say later) and for a process which involves identifying problems, exploring possible resolutions, sharing responsibility for learning and outcome and for working together. We believe these ways of working should apply to both research and intervention in marriage, as well as to the ways in which each informs the other. We hope that the book will make a contribution to planning and action as well as to the principles and practices governing work with couples.

Researchers and practitioners use different terms to describe the people with whom they work. Within the organizations in which we have been employed the terms 'patient' or 'client' are used to describe those who seek help or are referred by another professional or agency for help. They describe a state, a role, a relationship, often vaguely and with a taken-for-granted, unexamined meaning. Even when loosely used such terms define and determine to a significant degree the nature and course of the interaction between patient and doctor or client and counsellor. They are terms which are containing, in the positive sense that they put a limit on what is possible, acceptable, realistic. At the same time they are constraining, in the more negative sense of restricting that which is possible, of limiting potential. The same is true of 'research subjects', those who willingly or otherwise, with or without consent, are the focus of the researcher's interest. The description is of someone or some group potentially important to the researcher, and through whose cooperation questions are answered and ideas tested. Both in the formal literature and in day-to-day practice patients, clients and research subjects may have attributed to them a variety of drives, functions, behaviours, attitudes, with varying symptoms or defensive mechanisms. We find these terms limiting and at times unhelpful. Too much emphasis on parts risks a neglect of the whole; too much attention to role risks overlooking those who undertake it; too much attention to attitudes risks denying the complexity of thoughts and feelings. We shall therefore be concerned throughout with the *person*, using the term to seek to convey a sense of totalness, of each individual being always herself or himself, however incompletely at any one time. Gender is an important part of this discourse, and so we shall refer often to 'husbands' and 'wives', avoiding for the most part the particular connotations of the term *partner*. Full person-ness we see as self-in-relation-to-others, a state and a process in which self grows, evolves, becomes defined and when all is well, becomes a responsible free agent, an independent, autonomous, relating 'I'. To work together with patients, clients, research subjects in this way loosens constraints, extends potential and of course produces certain risks.

The variables of both time and space will be important to us in these explorations. Our time perspective about marital relationships is that of at least a lifetime, in the sense that most adults who enter into matrimony will remain married to their first spouse for the greater part of their lives; and for those who do not, but who may divorce, remarry and/or cohabit, the greater part of their lives is still likely to be spent in some form of marital relationship. Our time scale is also of more than one generation, because almost all marriages, all marital relationships, are affected by at least two marriages in the previous generation and most marriages will affect the succeeding generation. As we shall show, the 'life time' of marriage has extended considerably since the mid-nineteenth century, with a number of personal and institutional consequences.

Space and the boundaries which define it are also important dimensions in our thinking about marriage. Here we refer perhaps more to metaphor than to any objectively measurable reality. We are thinking about the boundaries which define and contribute to the identity of persons, of the space between persons, of the space between identifiably separate selves, in which takes place those interactions which confirm individual identities and give shape and meaning to the relationship between them. Such ideas have relevance to the development of mother-child, husband-wife experience, and also to those encounters which are called therapeutic. These ideas, which owe much to the object relations school, we will elaborate in part 3 of the book.

From a sociological perspective, our primary debt is to C. Wright Mills (1959) and his classic distinction between 'private troubles' and 'public issues'. For the couple in marital distress, the difficulties which are encountered may often appear as unique, personal traumas which are the highly individual product of private experience. At one level of course, this is exactly the case and it may be the task of the sociologist in the research setting, or of the therapist in the context of the helping relationship, to make sense of this. But at another level this unique private trouble is also a constituent element in a more complex public issue. When, for example, the incidence of marital break-up in a society reaches levels that have a major effect on rates of divorce and remarriage, then this has consequences for a variety of other elements within the social structure: housing and labour markets, welfare services, benefits systems and the political economy in general. When this distinction between private and public is set in a temporal context, we are also dealing with Wright Mills' other concern, the integration of biography and history. Each of these dimensions, of personal time and social time, must be taken account of by those who seek to investigate or to intervene in the marital relationship. We shall therefore be much concerned here with the exploration of personal problems in their structural and historical context.

It should be clear from this that we do not have in mind a restricted range of readers; for example, those of a particular profession or discipline, or those working in specific organizations and agencies. We hope the book will be of interest to a wide spread of people who have a professional interest in working with couples, as well as those who are interested more generally in marriage, family life and personal relationships. Our intention is to start a discussion among this readership and hope that it will be carried forward by those working in research, medicine, social work and counselling, as well as those involved in family therapy and some of the newer agencies concerned with conciliation, and with stepfamilies. We shall try to do this by exploring the concept of consultation, which we believe should be common to all of them. We are aware in this that we risk a blurring of focus, superficiality, satisfying no particular group of readers, even appearing to lack a clear commitment. We are prepared to take this risk in the belief that our book will avoid the fragmentation, the partiality, the polarization of much recent writing on marriage and its problems.

1.2 Focusing on Marriage

Few people would deny that in recent years we have witnessed in our culture a growing public debate about family life and relationships within the family. This has ranged from a variety of feminist critiques of the family as the primary site of gender divisions in our society, through contributions from both the political left and right on the role of the family and the state in the care of the individual, to wide-ranging debate about the social and personal consequences of what is now generally accepted as mass levels of divorce. The popular media appear to have an insatiable appetite for stories and features on subjects like cohabitation, marital break-up, stepfamilies and single parents, while the highly complex issue of child abuse is rarely far from the headlines. Amidst all this discussion we have continued to engage with and be intrigued by a significant gap. We have found that questions about the institution and the relationship called marriage, and the links between them, are rarely addressed in any sustained manner by either reseachers or practitioners. Policy-makers and politicians, for their part, seldom engage with the subject, though they may be assiduous in defending or blaming 'the family' in relation to some topical issue or other. It is almost as if marriage has become some kind of taboo, recognized as existing all around us, but rarely exposed to serious scrutiny. There is an important lesson to be learned from this, for it underlines the way in which the subject of this book opens up a boundary which many prefer to remain closed: that between the personal and the professional. Marriage, marital problems and the pain and rewards of adult heterosexual couple relationships are in the main not subjects for open discussion; for most of us it is far easier to talk about social trends relating to marriage, or the marriage problems of others, than to recognize that to be married is to constitute part of the trend and to experience some of the consequences.

This paradox is reflected even in some of the organizations which, to the casual observer, may appear to be unequivocally concerned with marriage. Members of the various marriage guidance councils have debated for some time the extent to which they should remain as services dedicated to marriage. Much energy has gone into the question of whether the word 'marriage' should continue to figure so prominently in their name when, for example, work is carried out with persons who are not married, or with those who are divorcing. Even in the time that we have been writing this book the National Marriage Guidance Council has relaunched its service under the new name of Relate, a process to which we shall return at greater length in part 4. It is by no means clear therefore whether the marital agencies exist solely to help those in marriage; whether they seek actively to promote the institution of marriage; or whether their services are offered more generally in the context of a wide range of differing 'personal relationships'.

We are therefore concerned here to maintain a focus on marriage, as an issue which raises important questions for research, for practice and for the organization of services. We do not seek to do this in some narrow, defensive way. We do however believe that the ubiquity of marriage and divorce in our society calls for them to be taken more seriously. How marital relationships are constituted or dissolved and how problems within them are resolved are crucial questions. They are relevant not only to the researcher and the practitioner, but also to the policy-maker and the politician.

Having said this, we should add that we do not wish in any sense to 'privilege' marriage and we certainly do not seek to imply that it has any innate or natural qualities that make it superior to other forms of adult relationship. In terms of heterosexual relationships, while acknowledging differences between marriages by habit and repute, common-law marriages and cohabitation, we also note how frequently these are indistinguishable from institutional marriage. Likewise, gay and lesbian relationships demand consideration, not as examples of deviant behaviour, but of different choices which in turn point up, throw into relief and raise new questions about marriage itself. In the context of a plurality of adult relationships it must be recognized that not only are there many forms of marriage, but also that there are many alternatives to it. Among those who opt for alternatives, it is also significant that there may be a certain amount of movement back and forth between marital and nonmarital forms of relationship during the life course. For the present however, marriage, problems of marriage and marital relationships are our subjects, and it is upon these that we hope to maintain our focus.

1.3 Wedlocked?

Our title is intended to be more than a play on words, though its attraction also lies in the possibility of interpretation, of resonance and of ambiguity. At one level wedlock is a relationship involving a pledge or promise, one to the other. With the question mark we seek to relativize this, recognizing that pledges may be broken, may change over time and may mean different things to different individuals, particularly between men and women. Wedlock in this sceptical sense conveys issues of freedom or bondage; of being caught in unchanging stasis or being actively held; of acting upon the world or being acted upon. We think the term draws attention to paradox and polarities; to structures and processes; to possibilities and limitations which characterize the marital world.

Crucially, the idea of wedlock brings together two very separate realms of discourse about marriage. On the one hand there is that which is concerned with choosing, with giving meaning, with interpreting, with the realization and achievement of life goals through the marital relationship. This element of wedlock finds echoes in humanistic theories of the social, and constitutes an important theoretical underpinning to numerous schools of counselling, as well as to symbolic interactionism in sociology. It sees the human actor as implicitly rational, capable of control and empowered with the ability not only to make sense of the social world, but also to shape and mould it according to the requirements of circumstance and contingency. By contrast, the other side of wedlock emphasizes structures, constraints, rules, roles and penalties. Here, to be married is to submit to one's partner, to the culture and to the controlling powers of the wider society. Mechanical, rather than organic imagery is most appropriate to this form of wedlock, which channels individuals along pre-determined routes and which numbs creativity at the expense of order, control and conservatism.

Wedlocked? then is a metaphor wherein sociologist and psychotherapist can seek to develop a common language; one which draws together rather than polarizes and which emphasizes the potentially creative space between, rather than the differences which maintain separation. Here are possibilities for researcher and practitioner, for working with the public and private, the outer and the inner, the professional and the personal. It is these aspects of marriage which we seek to explore. We have therefore thought carefully about how our text should be organized, and concluded that a structure based on parts, rather than chapters, would be most appropriate. By organizing the material in this way it has been possible to explore various aspects of our main themes, in particular by looking at the ways in which researchers and practitioners may have differing, complementary or even conflicting positions and understandings. We conclude this introductory part, with a brief outline of what is to follow in further parts of the book.

In part 2 our focus is on the sociological dimensions of marriage, looked at from the perspective of the life course. We begin by examining changing beliefs and ideologies about marriage, showing how these may be linked to wider arrangements within the social structure. In recent years there has been an increasing willingness in some quarters to view changes in marriage from a *pluralist* perspective, which emphasizes the role of individual choice and sees marriage as a 'project' which can be fashioned according to the desires of the spouses. We find this notion both helpful in emphasizing the *social construction* of the marital world, but also unrealistic in ignoring the extent to which freedom and choice may be affected by a range of sociological factors. We therefore go on to explore the dimensions of life expectancy, gender, health, cohabitation, fertility, employment and unemployment and social class, looking for ways in which they may act as sources of marital variation. Sociologists have written little about *marital problems*; we try to locate this category of phenomena in a wider historical and cultural perspective, paying particular attention to what it may tell us about gender differences. We look at various sorts of accounts of marital problems and of marriage break-up. Variations in rates of divorce are described and are linked to changes in the law. We conclude by exploring the issues of remarriage, looking at pathways into a second or subsequent marriage and examining the ways in which marriage after divorce is shaped by the emotional and material legacies of the past. Throughout part 2 we are at pains to emphasize that marriage is both institution *and* relationship; an adequate sociological account of marriage is therefore one which is able to pay attention to both structure and process, showing how the meaning of marital relationships within society is shaped by a wide range of external and internal factors.

This theme of outer and inner worlds is further developed in part 3, principally from the viewpoint of the therapist. We begin with an exploration of some existential realities and of opportunities and obligations, within the long-term heterosexual relationship of marriage. We look at some of the developmental aspects of marriage through the life course and the processes by which particular kinds of couples develop particular problems in their relationship; we use a model of causation which is historical and developmental, dynamic and contextual. This leads us to a variety of issues in intervention. We offer a brief account of the psychodynamic, behavioural, existential and systems models as they are applied to marital work. Ethical issues in practice are discussed as they relate to such themes as practitioners' competency, the goals of intervention, neutrality and confidentiality. We then introduce our own model for intervention, that of *consultation*, explaining its conceptual underpinnings. A number of sections deal with the practice of consultation, exploring in particular the first encounter between couple and consultant and the content and process of subsequent work. We offer some guidelines about the organization of such work, ranging from the setting in which it takes place, to issues of contracting, review and closure. We emphasize throughout the notion of couple and consultant taking joint responsibility for the work, though paying careful attention to their very different experiences of the consultation process. It is suggested that the model of consultation has particular advantages in allowing the focus on the couple relationship to be developed and maintained.

In part 4 we turn our attention to the organizational contexts in which both research and intervention take place. We start by reviewing the work of the main marital agencies, some of which are currently undergoing major changes, and we also look at marital work in the statutory health and social services, concluding with some reference to the more recent developments which have taken place in the field of conciliation. Much of our thinking about all of these agencies has been set against the recommendations which appeared in *Marriage Matters*. The extent to which and reasons why these recommendations have not been implemented is an important theme running through part 4; we are on the whole pessimistic about the possibilities for future development. An examination of issues in practice takes us into discussion about the ways in which counsellors and therapists are selected, trained and supervised; we look at the personal and professional problems which face those who undertake marital work. Our focus then turns to the issue of research into marriage and marital work. We distinguish between two strands of *formal* and *applied* work in this area. We show that the organizational links between research, practice and training in marital work are on the whole very weak. Encouragingly, however, social researchers have shown a growing interest in recent years in studying aspects of marriage, divorce and remarriage; we describe a developing corpus of this work, much of which relies on the use of qualitative methods. Although one of the aims of such research is to provide detailed accounts of intimate life within the terms of reference of the research subjects, we have been disappointed to find that researchers have not in general shown a willingness to draw on the practical and conceptual experience of therapists and counsellors. There is clearly an important overlap area here, where issues in the management and analysis of interviews and questions of ethics and of confidentiality are all of mutual interest and concern to both researchers and practitioners. Similarly, when we turn to more applied research into marital work, we find that this has for the most part been conducted by practitioners and has in general not benefited from the wider perspective and skills of social researchers. Part 4 should therefore be read as a critical commentary on the existing organizational arrangements for the development of research and intervention in marriage.

Part 5 begins with a reiteration of the problems which are encountered in seeking to keep the focus of attention on marriage, rather than wider aspects of family and domestic life. This is a dilemma common to both research and intervention, where in each case there are temptations to move away from marriage, as both institution and relationship, into some wider territory. We look at the relationship between marriage, marital problems and social policy, asking why the subject of marriage seems to occupy such an ambivalent place within political debate. This ambivalence is also reflected in the practice of a wide range of professionals who regard intervention in marriage as essentially a 'no-go area'. It seems unlikely that there will be any significant expansion in the amount of marital work undertaken in the statutory caring services; this leaves the voluntary agencies as the main service providers, albeit severely restricted by government policies of limiting state support for such organizations. Within this climate of paradox and restraint, of economic and political uncertainty, we suggest that the main prospect for development lies in greater collaboration between reseachers and practitioners and in more consultative approaches to the development of services. At relatively little material cost, there is the potential for a good deal of learning to result from therapists, counsellors, consultants and researchers coming together for the exchange of ideas, concerns and problems. Likewise, there are possibilities for more flexible forms of service to couples, based on notions of self-empowerment and community development; though these principles have underpinned initiatives in working with a wide range of other personal and health problems, they have yet to be applied with any degree of commitment to marital problems. We conclude that such developments are achievable within the context of a broadly consultative approach to both research and intervention in marriage.

2

Processes and Structures in Marriage through the Life Course

In this part of the book we shall be reviewing a wide range of material on marriage, seeking throughout to maintain a balance between questions of *structure* and *process*. For whereas it is certainly important to form an appreciation of the major social divisions relating to marriage, it is also the case that these are changing over time and that *social trends* are themselves products of individual human relations. In general terms we believe that social inquiry should always be alert to the continuities and interactions between the world of individual experience and the broader context of social structure.

A series of underlying themes will be present throughout this discussion of sociological aspects of marriage. Our concern will be to examine those ways in which marriage in our culture may be constituted, dissolved and reconstituted over time. This is not merely to explore the phenomena of marriage, divorce and remarriage, though these are clearly of major importance. It is also to address that majority still of all marriages which endure until the death of one of the partners, and to ask how these relationships may be constituted, dissolved and reconstituted over decades and generations.

In doing this we shall be at pains to avoid the use of concepts and terminology which imply that such processes are inevitable and are somehow irretrievably linked to a progression through a series of life stages. Of course it is helpful to consider categories such as 'courtship', 'early marriage', 'the first baby', 'teenage children' and so forth; but it is a great mistake to assume that such stages are either inevitable or 'natural', and certainly quite wrong to imply that deviations from them are pathological. The experience of constituting, dissolving and reconstituting the marital world, whether with the same or more than one partner, must in our view be seen in a wider context, that of the *life course*. Cohen has described the life course as being 'like a bus journey punctuated by stages, with boarding and embarkation points ... these stages are not fixed, have changed in length in response to wide social change, and ... new stages have emerged. The boarding and embarkation points for childhood youth or midlife have either lengthened or shortened over time and vary according to region and culture' (1987:3). Rather less prosaically, Morgan quotes Haraven's description of the life course as 'a shoal of fish moving through the water with fish breaking from one little cluster of fish to join another and then move on to a third, partially composed of previous swimming companions' (Morgan 1985:178). It is likewise our preference to see generations of married persons, as individuals, couples and groups displaying complex patterns of interrelationship, which need to be described and analysed on a number of levels, ranging from the socio-demographic to the ideological.

It is probably fair to say that a concern with aspects of constitution, dissolution and resolution in marriage is not one which would normally be associated with the discipline of academic sociology. Indeed, a first reaction to such terms is more likely to evoke resonances of their *clinical* nature. They are however of crucial importance to a sociological appraisal of changing aspects of marriage. Much of our understanding of how marriages are constituted, together with related expectations, remains clouded by assumptions and myths; and the process of becoming a 'couple' is poorly understood in the context of changing public moralities of marriage and partnership. Likewise, just as there is no unitary pattern of how the marriage relationship is formed, so the factors associated with its dissolution vary widely and lead to a range of effects, both personal and social. The resolution of tension within marriage can also take a number of forms, of which divorce is only the most obvious and the most visible. The marital life course should therefore be seen as multilayered and many-stranded, but containing a range of core themes which occur and recur.

2.1 Ideologies of Marriage and Partnership

YOUNG PEOPLE AND MARRIAGE

For a time in the 1960s it was as if young people had gained a monopoly on marriage. Products of the postwar baby bulge, now young adults, were entering matrimony in unprecedented numbers and at ages often considered youthful and premature by the standards of their parents' generation. Recalling the press reports of the time, this was the age of 'gym-slip mums' and 'teenage brides'. Later, this cohort of marriages was to attract further notoriety when it provided a significant proportion of the 'divorce boom' of the mid- to late 1970s. For a while however, young people and marriage were centre stage in the popular debate, puzzling epiphenomena of those years in which so many aspects of personal life and private morality were called into question, redefined or rejected: what Weeks (1981) has called 'the permissive moment'.

It would be hard to dispute the assertion that the 1960s proved a watershed in the history of family life, marriage and personal relationships in Britain. Liberalization of the divorce laws, new legislation on abortion and homosexuality and a growing awareness among politicians of the concerns of young people (fired no doubt by its vote-catching potential) all served to differentiate these years from the ideologically undemanding decade of the 1950s, when Britain's family policy had settled into a cosy, post-Beveridge complacency.

The paradox is that rebellious youth should have sought out the institution of marriage so assiduously. By 1972 one in three spinsters marrying was a teenager (CSO 1985:36). One-third of teenage brides in 1969–70 were pregnant and 43 per cent of all births conceived premaritally were to teenage mothers (Ineichen 1977:55). These young women were predominantly from social classes IV and V. Precipitated marriage and low social class became a well-known correlate of divorce (Gibson, 1974; Thornes and Collard 1979:80). Young brides also shared a number of other disadvantages, being more likely to start married life in shared accommodation, and, if not already pregnant, more likely than their older counterparts to have a baby at an early stage of their marriage, and having done so, to go on to produce a greater number of subsequent children. Such trends raised questions about the pressures on those involved. Worryingly, for the social analyst, they suggested a lemming-like rush into what one writer called 'the vortex of disadvantage' (Ineichen 1977).

In the intervening years since the late 1960s, marriage has been subjected to new forms of critical scrutiny. Its naturalness and given-ness have been challenged by those who see clear social and historical processes at work in the taken-for-granted world of family life. Rates of marriage, especially among young people, have fallen and levels of cohabitation have increased. Between 1981 and 1982 numbers of teenage brides fell by 13 per cent; and between the mid-

and late 1970s premarital cohabitation rose sharply. Meanwhile a 1980s generation of young people emerged, their adolescence tempered by recession and unemployment, rather than by consumer-led affluence. This new generation appeared on the one hand sceptical of marriage and on the other sought from it increasingly high levels of personal satisfaction and fulfilment. The differences are largely explicable in structural terms.

A number of writers (Coffield 1987; Willis 1977) have provided us with portrayals of the harshness of early adulthood for those living in areas of high unemployment. Coffield describes a generation of young working-class women and men in North East England, pushed from pillar to post of various employment schemes, dejected, disillusioned and with limited psychological resources to construct stratagems for alternative life styles. 'Neither prolonged personal experience of unemployment, nor controversial calls for the right to useful unemployment . . . nor arguments in favour of a move to a "life ethic" . . . in any way shook the attachment of young adults to the Protestant work ethic' (Coffield 1987:96). Such remarks bear testimony to the significance of the wage as a pivot around which turn subsequent life plans for getting married, setting up a home and exercising some power in the consumer market (Willis 1984:476). For this generation of young working-class people, life becomes a tortuous balancing act in which powerful cultural values are weighed against conflicting structural circumstances. The picture may be further complicated by a variety of other tensions: rows with parents; divided loyalties between peer group and spouse; and sheer frustration at the absence of cash and spending power. Such basic features cannot be isolated from changing beliefs and ideologies about marriage and domestic life. The hubris which surrounded personal relationships in the 1960s, underpinned by economic buoyancy and greater spending power, was massively eroded for some groups in the 1980s.

MARRIAGE AND THE CONSTRUCTION OF REALITY

Now this is a far cry from the way in which sociologists had described the meanings of married life in the 1960s. Berger and Kellner's famous humanistic account of marriage as a shield against anomie proves rather difficult reading only 25 years later:

Marriage in our society is a *dramatic* event in which two strangers come together and redefine themselves. The drama of the act is internally anticipated and socially legitimated long before it takes place in the individual's biography, and amplified by a pervasive ideology, the dominant themes of which (romantic love, sexual fulfilment, self-discovery and self-realization through love and sexuality, the nuclear family as the social site for these processes) can be found distributed through all strata of the society. (Berger and Kellner 1964:5)

In addition to being empirically challengeable, such statements are laden with their own ideological assumptions about what does and should constitute the marriage relationship in our society. Accordingly, Berger and Kellner's view of marriage as a 'nomos building instrumentality' (1964:1) in which the partners, through conversation with one another, construct a micro-world which is meaningful to them, both individually and as a couple, has engendered a number of criticisms.

Berger and Kellner have been accused of ignoring 'the effects which macro-structures have on everyday life, and more specifically, the ways in which structural factors determine how the expectations and experiences of men and women will differ in marriage' (Burgoyne and Clark 1984:10). For Askham, Berger and Kellner fail to take account of a fundamental contradiction within marriage, which can act as a source of *both* identity and stability (Askham 1984:5). Most fundamentally of all, for Morgan, Berger and Kellner's is a position which overemphasizes the relational aspects of marriage at the expense of the structural (Morgan 1982).

Nevertheless, the Berger and Kellner thesis has been of enormous importance, and though many have shaken off the suffocating language in which it was couched, along with its ponderous pretensions to meta-theory, the message lingers on and has informed the research practice of a generation of sociologists. It is no longer necessary to take on board the full implications and consequences of the Berger and Kellner sociology of knowledge in order to accept the principle that marriage must be seen as a dynamic entity in which to some extent there is the possibility of self-understanding and personal growth; remembering always that it is also an institution which connects at a number of levels – legal, moral, fiscal, economic – with a wider social apparatus. In this respect Berger and Kellner were of major importance in liberating family sociology from the functionalism of Talcott Parsons (Parsons and Bales 1956) which had reduced the modern, isolated nuclear family to two key tasks: the *socialization* of children and the *stabilization* of adult personalities. Without that contribution, the only available antidote to Parsons within the discipline of sociology would have been a crude Marxism, capable of seeing the family simply as a site for the reproduction of capitalist relations, but blind and hostile to its importance as a source of meaning.

Berger and Kellner also created an intellectual space in which other social theorists and commentators were able to develop new ideas in relation to marriage and family life. The work of both Sennett (1974) and Lasch (1977) may be seen in this context. Both writers assume a process of *privatization* within Western societies which reduces the role of public existence and of citizenry and which devalues it in favour of more circumscribed life goals located in the sphere of home, family and friends. This process is regarded as an inevitable consequence of industrialization, which in creating the radical separation of home and workplace caused the external, public world to be seen in increasingly hostile terms – a place from which home and family could offer safety and protection. There are clearly some difficulties with regard to gender in this argument; implicit in the privatization thesis are certain assumptions about the role of men as key actors in the public world, while women confine themselves to matters of domesticity and kin. For Lasch however, the problem with the analysis is that the family itself is overrun and occupied by the outside forces of 'caring' professionals whose *therapeutic ideologies* have colonized family relationships, laying them bare to external scrutiny and control (Lasch 1977). This argument has been further developed by Donzelot (1980) who has shown how state interventions in the family, by social workers, doctors and what he calls the 'psy' forces, define the family's inability to carry out increasingly specialized functions and so render it ever weaker to invasion and control by state forces.

BELIEFS ABOUT MARRIAGE AND DIVORCE

It is important to understand however that subsequent changes in the sociological understanding of marriage have not been conducted solely at the level of detached theory; indeed there has been a growing interest in linking theories about marriage and the family to a clearer understanding of changing social trends; much of this has taken place in the context of debates about family policy and services. Faced with the sheer complexity of changing family and domestic patterns, some writers have sought refuge in a *pluralist* framework which portrays couples as consumers in a marketplace, freely selecting the lifestyle of their choice from a number of options. Such a position has obvious attractions to liberals who are keen to describe rising divorce rates in neutral tones and without recourse to polemic or reproach. In Britain the genre was championed by the Rapoports (1977) and institutionalized in the work of the Study Commission on the Family (1983). As we shall see, it is a position which appears to have had a major influence upon policy-makers, as well as on practitioners of marital counselling and therapy. Indeed, a pluralist view of contemporary marriage is also implicit in much *popular* comment, which recognizes the freedom of couples to self-determination, while avoiding the use of pathological or value-laden terms for the description of marital dissolution or divorce.

For others, changing patterns of marriage and divorce have posed more fundamental questions about the meaning of contemporary partnerships and the ways in which new trends might be experienced by the individuals and couples involved. It is in the work of these writers that some integration of public and private dimensions appears to take place. Studies of single parenthood (Marsden 1969; George and Wilding 1972) have provided detailed insights into the life worlds and material circumstances of both lone mothers and lone fathers. Processes of divorce and of postmarital experience have been explored by Hart (1976) and Chester (1971), and later in much more detail by Burgoyne and Clark (1984). While feminists focus on women's issues in relation to marriage and divorce (Smart 1984), others, particularly from social psychology, have charted new terri-tory with studies of aspects of fatherhood and masculinity (O'Brien and McKee 1982; Lewis and O'Brien 1987). The work of Finch (1983) has been of major importance in describing the interrelationships between marriage and employment and more recently Mattinson (1988) has produced a study of the ways in which marriages are affected by unemployment.

A number of these studies will be referred to later in more detail. For the moment they are important in reminding us of the serious attention which academic scholarship has given to changes taking place in both the institution and the relationship of marriage; and of the thinking of other opinion-formers who have shown a great willingness to comment on marriage and family issues: journalists, churchpeople and politicians in particular. This growing *public debate* has played a major part in shaping current beliefs about marriage in our society; at the very least it is important to keep in mind its boundaries when considering any issue of research or intervention in marriage.

For a time in the 1970s readers of the popular press might have been forgiven for thinking that the institution of marriage had largely been abandoned by a 'divorce-crazy Britain', which, aided by the relaxed legislation of 1969 in England and Wales and of 1976 in Scotland, was engaged en masse in throwing off the shackles of matrimony. Ironically, this apparent flight from marriage was accompanied by rhetorics which placed a far greater importance on the *quality* of marital relationships. Husband-wife relationships, for so long the stuff of music-hall jokes, suddenly became matters of deadly earnest. Agony columns proliferated, each dispensing its own brand of expert opinion on the circumstances in which a marriage could be deemed 'successful' or not, and each apparently raising the stakes to new heights of personal fulfilment.

A number of themes dominated the popular debate: sexuality, parenthood and gender relations, especially the domestic division of labour. The rhetoric of sexual freedom before marriage, if not within it, became a commonplace during the 1960s and 1970s; a plethora of magazines and popular books explored sexual issues with a candour never known before. This was closely related to issues of fertility control and the ability to determine the number of children in a family and to time their arrival. It was of course the 1960s which championed what Edmund Leach (1967) referred to as the 'cornflakes packet norm', of mother, father and two children. This 'nuclear family' (again a technical term which entered into popular discourse) however, stripped of its wider network, was a sweet and sour mixture in which personal growth and fulfilment could easily give way to dissatisfaction and disillusion. The negative side of these marriages was therefore the way in which they exposed inequalities between husbands and wives, particularly following the birth of a first child, when many a liberated couple suddenly appeared to revert back to type, forcing the female partner into a bygone role and laying up a variety of discontents for the future of the relationship. Writers like Cooper (1972) and Laing (1971) weighed in to this debate and their books sold in thousands, gaining a good deal of support from those who agreed that modern families and modern marriages were the key sites of mental illness and personal distress in our culture.

But this so-called radical psychiatry was quickly countervailed by liberal sociology, for which the social casualties of divorce were no more than the victims of their own high expectations. Rising divorce rates were a product of taking marriage more, rather than less seriously (Fletcher 1966). The institution of marriage was popular as never before; where it was under pressure then services should be developed to help those in need. The interdepartmental working party report on marriage guidance, *Marriage Matters* (1979), about which we shall have more to say in part 4, recognized that the state had some part to play in this. It addressed the *public* consequences – in ill health, absenteeism, support for single parents – of the *private* miseries of divorce. Such arguments fed back in turn into the popular debate and gained widespread currency. Though referrals to the marital agencies did not increase to anything like the expected levels, the *idea* of outside intervention in a troubled marriage did become more widely acceptable and was certainly promoted by advice-givers in newspapers and magazines, who were increasingly likely to recommend the services of marriage guidance councils to readers.

There is a sense in which these arguments served to highlight the processual aspects of marriage and divorce; this was further rein-forced by a variety of soap opera and popular drama scripts which introduced marital problems and divorce issues to a mass audience. Divorce became less stigmatizing, at least on a public level, and was less likely to be associated with characteristics of personal inadequa-cy. Whereas divorce had formerly been confined to the privileged rich or the dissolute poor (though for the latter, usually in the guise of informal separation) it now became more widespread, though still selectively, through the class structure. By the early 1980s divorce had become a mass phenomenon, intrinsic to our understanding of marriage and partnership and related expectations, but still poorly understood in its aetiology and consequences. Certain key trends had crystallized however, in the light of which a detailed analysis of the public and private dimensions of the marital world became possible.

2.2 Sources of Marital Variation

Whatever the level or intensity of our interest, most of us are aware that in recent decades a number of important changes have taken place in patterns of marriage, divorce and remarriage. For the researcher, counsellor or therapist however it is particularly impor-tant to have a clear conception of the status of these changes, and to know how to interpret them. It is not necessary here for us to go into great demographic detail; this has been ably summarized elsewhere (Rimmer 1981) and current information is readily available from government sources. Instead we list a catalogue of key trends. Our intention is that it should serve as an introduction to a range of topics which reveal how the marital world is fragmented, and which highlights both the commonalities and the differing experiences of those who live out some part of their lives in the state of wedlock. The very universality of marriage within our culture means that it also has the potential to contain a wide range of variation in material and economic circumstances. Before proceeding to that discussion however, and at the risk of causing offence to demographic purists, we list a summary of the main patterns.

1   About 390,000 marriages occur in Britain each year. Some 85 per cent of men and 91 per cent of women will marry at some point in their lives. Rates of marriage in our society have steadily increased throughout the twentieth century, but have begun to fall in recent years. The rate of marriage is usually expressed as the number per thousand of the eligible population who marry in a given year, which may vary even though the rate remains constant. Overall, rates of marriage would be falling more rapidly if it were not for the propensity of divorced persons to marry again; rates of first marriage are in the sharpest decline. Around 90 per cent of those who marry have children.

2   It remains unclear how far falling marriage rates are a feature of the increased propensity to cohabit. Cohabitation is more popular, but seems to be delaying matrimony rather than replacing it.

3   The number of divorces taking place in Britain increased around fivefold between 1960 and 1980. On present trends about a third of marriages now taking place are likely to end in divorce: this does not mean that a third of all marriages now in existence will end in this way. Indeed, the proportion of divorced men and women in the adult population is very small – in the region of 5 per cent. Rates of divorce have been fairly constant in recent years, though they are highest in England and Wales, lower in Scotland and lowest of all in Northern Ireland. There are about 160,000 divorces each year in Britain.

4   The most common time for divorce to occur is in the eighth year of marriage. Some six out of ten divorces involve children under 16. Around 90 per cent of these continue to live with their mothers.

5   Approximately one marriage in three is now a remarriage for one or other partner. The most common form of remarriage in England and Wales is between two divorced partners; in Scotland it is between a divorced man and a spinster. Some 50 per cent of divorced men and women remarry within five years. However, rates of remarriage are nearly three times higher among divorced men than among divorced women. There are about 120,000 remarriages each year in Britain.

These trends are in turn interconnected with a wide range of other variables relating to distinct experiences in the process of getting married, divorcing and remarrying. In the subsections which follow we shall explore variations in life expectancy, gender and sexuality, health, cohabitation, patterns of childbearing, employment, class and culture.

LIFE EXPECTANCY

In 1851 the average expectancy of life in Britain was 40 years for men and 42 years for women. A hundred years later these figures had increased to 66 and 71, respectively. By the mid-1980s they had reached 70 and 76 (Dominian 1980:13; Burgoyne 1987). These changes in life expectancy have significant implications when considered alongside parallel changes in age at marriage. At the beginning of this century the mean age at marriage was 27.2 years for bachelors and 25.6 years for spinsters. By 1983 bachelors were marrying at an average age of 25.7 and spinsters at 23.4 (Rimmer 1981:17; OPCS 1984). In other words, over the last century and a half we have been living longer and marrying younger. So for those who ever marry, and that is perhaps 90 per cent of the population on recent estimates, the expected duration of marriage to death is higher than ever before, at all ages (Nissel 1987).

These demographic changes have profound consequences for the way in which we might think about marriage, and yet it is as if they have failed to percolate through to belief and value systems surrounding the marriage relationship, which remains idealized as lifelong and monogamous. ''Til death us do part' means something very different now to what it did for our mid-Victorian forebears. Today's newly-weds, if they remain married to one another (and two-thirds do) can expect a relationship, a set of duties, obligations and responsibilities which may last 50 years or more.

This extended marital life course remains poorly understood and most sociological inquiry directed towards it has been somewhat 'front-loaded', concentrating on the early phases of married life rather than the mid- or later years. With the exception of some important work by Mason (1987), sociologists have shown very little interest in studying the married life of elderly people, despite the fact that post-retiral couples now constitute a larger proportion of the population than ever before. Accordingly, there is no clear picture to be obtained from the literature about levels of marital satisfaction over the life course, though a commonly propounded thesis (James and

Wilson 1986:31) is one showing a gradual increase in levels of satisfaction following the departure of children (albeit never reaching those levels enjoyed by the couple during the initial child-free period of their relationship), which continues into later life until such time as illness and/or death of a spouse produces renewed decline.

Of course, *retirement* is likely to have a marked effect upon the couple and may have very different implications for men and women. It is an event which can produce a profound reappraisal of the marital relationship for some couples, perhaps resulting in such things as the renegotiation of the domestic division of labour, money management, leisure-time pursuits and contacts with wider social networks. But as a professor of general practice once remarked, retirement can also produce a 'toxic overdose' of one's partner, especially in cases where the couple have hitherto led rather separate lives. The couple dimension may also have an influence on other factors, such as housing requirements and patterns of migration in later life. The decision whether or not to relocate at the time of retirement may be determined both by the material resources of the couple, including access to support networks, and also by their self-image, the way they see their relationship and the type of marriage they hope to enjoy in later life.

Increased longevity and the prospect of longer marriages also raise numerous questions about dependency and informal caring. Very elderly parents may continue to be looked after even when their offspring are themselves beyond retirement age. It is most likely that the major burden of this form of care will fall upon the female members of the family. Wives are in turn more likely to stay healthier than and outlive their husbands and to face the problems of caring for them during periods of illness and physical decline. It seems likely that such responsibilities may also create pressures within the marital relationship in later life (Mason 1987). It is perhaps a result of the powerful stereotypes which surround marriage in this phase that there has been so little interest shown in it by sociologists. Our observation is that older couples themselves are also unlikely to seek help from the caring agencies and are probably seen only infrequently by marital therapists. For researcher and therapist alike these marriages therefore create major interpretive problems, and call for sensitivity in the use of a life course perspective.

GENDER AND SEXUALITY

It is largely as a result of the attentions of feminist theory and practice that the sociological study of marriage and family life has enjoyed something of a revival in recent years. It would be quite impossible to attempt a summary of this work here; not only has feminism revived substantive interest in family and domestic life, it has also generated a range of theoretical and methodological questions which create a major break from an earlier generation of sociological studies conducted during the 1950s and early 1960s. Actually many feminists would eschew an alignment with the sociological tradition as such, arguing that feminism integrates a range of disciplinary perspectives around a unifying theme of female oppression and exploitation. Marriage is frequently regarded as a key site of these experiences.

It was Jessie Bernard (1973) who first encouraged us to consider the *two* marriages, his and hers, which exist inside every marital 'partnership'. This simple assertion of a gendered difference in expectations, rewards, obligations and duties opened up new avenues of social inquiry into marriage. Men and women 'explain' themselves in different ways, arising out of their contrasting biographies and socially constructed attributes. The marriage relationship frequently holds a mirror to these differences, allowing us to see in microcosm the ways in which men and women, even when of like class, region or ethnic origin, may have radically differing experiences of the world. A range of studies has gone on to develop a specifically feminist perspective on such issues as housework (Gavron 1968; Oakley 1974), divorce (Smart 1984), employment (Finch 1983) and violence (Pahl 1985).

The feminist tradition has also benefited from new work by historians. As Davidoff has recently pointed out, 'It is a truism of social history that the last fifteen years has been a boom period for research and publication in that area which used to be regarded as "private life": the family, marriage, sexuality and romantic love' (1988:174). Whereas writers such as Macfarlane (1987) and Gillis (1985) have concentrated on broad historical sweeps covering patterns of reproduction or the ritual celebration of marriage from the fourteenth century onwards, others have concentrated upon marriage and divorce in the Victorian period (Horstman 1985; Mintz 1983; Davidoff and Hall 1987). Jane Lewis, for example, has alerted us to gender differences in marriage in the nineteenth century, showing how many working-class marriages in the 1870s turned around a set of 'financial obligations, services and activities that were gender specific' in relationships which 'did not enjoin romantic love or verbal and sexual intimacy' (Lewis 1984:9). This separation of male and female worlds was even more visible in the Victorian middle class, where the wife was subjected to total confinement in the private world of home and family: 'the angel in the household', dependent, passive and sexually innocent (Lewis 1984:77). Victorian husbands, by contrast, moved back and forth between public and private worlds and frequently enjoyed the moral latitude of the double standard.

It is often supposed that twentieth-century changes in patterns of women's education and employment have diminished these gender and class differences. After World War II, images of marital 'partnership', such as those promoted by Beveridge (Lewis 1984) were based upon a notion of differing, but complementary tasks, in which both husband and wife made their own unique contribution to the success of the relationship. This was much elaborated in Parsons and Bales' (1956) functional theory of modern marriage, where husbands played largely 'instrumental' roles which neatly dovetailed with their wives' 'affective' contributions, as nurturers and carers. Ironically, such conceptions of 'partnership', which are based on the implicit 'naturalness' of these gender divisions, continue to reinforce the separateness of male and female experiences of marriage, despite a veneer of congruence or 'symmetricality' (Young and Willmott 1975) in family roles.

Visible evidence of these continuing differences and inequalities is most clearly revealed when we turn to those areas of life which connect the married couple to the wider social structure. Men frequently experience and see marriage as something that supports them in the world of work, providing the domestic back-up which makes their working lives easier, and may even enhance their job prospects. They will expect this process to begin when they get married, often with 'wife' taking over where 'mother' left off, and to go on uninterrupted. Men are also likely to define certain areas of the domestic work as their own and jealously guard them as unequivocally male preserves: car mending, lawn mowing, do-it-yourself and so on. By contrast, when women get married they are likely to experience immediate tensions between the demands of paid work outside, and those of their unpaid labours inside the home. These will not only be pressures of time and physical energy; housework and cooking are also 'moral' categories which 'say something' about a woman's feelings for her husband and their marriage and which communicate to significant others such as parents, siblings and friends.

This double burden is unlikely to be shed by the woman, unless some major renegotiation takes place within the marriage. Instead it may be further amplified by the apparently 'joint' decision to start a family, which still means for the majority of women some break in paid employment in order to have children, followed by a return to lower-status work later (Martin and Roberts 1984). Although women are now more likely to return to paid work, usually part-time, between having babies and to go back to full-time work more quickly after their families are completed, it is still taken for granted within our culture that women's paid employment will take a backseat for some time during the child-bearing years.

There is however some evidence of change in the frequency and type of involvement which men experience in looking after their children. A recent major British survey found one half of women of the opinion that their husbands shared equally in the daily child care and the majority thought that their husbands were more likely to participate in child care than any other form of domestic work (Martin and Roberts 1984). An unprecedented recent change is that of fathers' presence at the birth of their children, which now occurs in the large majority of cases. It is important to get behind these trends and explore some of the changes in relationships which may underpin them. Richman's study of new fathers (1982) reveals how the birth of a baby may produce important opportunities for men to acknowledge their feelings and emotions. But another study by Smith and Simms (1982) has shown this may be a temporary phenomenon which is quickly circumscribed by the pressures of paid employment and working hours, often exacerbated by increased financial responsibilities.

Ironically, it has been studies of *stepfathers* (Burgoyne and Clark 1982) or *lone* fathers (Hipgrave 1982) which have told us a good deal about the meaning of fatherhood in our society. The father who becomes the stepparent to someone else's children, or the sole carer of his own, frequently encounters situations in which the underlying and taken-for-granted assumptions about fatherhood are graphically exposed and perhaps called into question. These themes have been successfully explored in a number of popular films, as well as in television drama and documentary, and in recent years the rights of fathers following divorce have been championed by a number of pressure groups. Fatherhood as a conscious, participative activity has thus become one of the idealizations of family life in our culture. Although we are still unsure of its form and extent, 'involved' fatherhood certainly occupies a place in popular consciousness, not least as it is reflected in media coverage of well-known 'father' personalities, from members of the royal family at one extreme, to rock musicians at the other.

Some of this is also linked to another preoccupation of social commentators: the 'new man'. A spate of recent books on aspects of male psychology has portrayed 'traditional' men as emotionally fragile and defended, unable to recognize or acknowledge their feelings and preserved in this insecure state by the cultural and ideological supports of male toughness and independence (Blackie and Clark 1987). These men lack friendships which are not linked to sexual gratification and so when they lose one frequently lose the other. They will tend to define marriage in terms of *role* rather than *relationship* and are likely to find difficulties in living independently if the marriage ends in divorce. 'New men', by contrast, have egalitarian relationships, characterized by mutuality and sharing; they also feel able to blur or reverse traditional domestic roles and can acknowledge personal talents or interests which are at variance with 'traditional' images of masculinity. Whether or not these 'new men' exist in substantial numbers is unclear; it would be helpful to know more.

Finally, we need to acknowledge the growing influence exerted upon such debates by an increasing awareness of issues of sexuality in society, particularly gay and lesbian relationships. A number of studies from Masters and Johnson (1966) onwards indicate that it is unwise to divide the world too arbitrarily into 'heterosexual' and 'homosexual'; up to a third of adult men and women may have engaged in sexual activity with other members of the same sex. Moreover, gay life styles and relationships have increasingly been championed as radical alternatives to heterosexual orthodoxy, offering other forms of expression, fulfilment and commitment. Growing public concern about the human immunodeficiency virus (HIV) and acquired immune deficiency syndrome (AIDS) has of course had an extremely negative influence upon these processes, producing in some countries highly visible moral panics, accompanied by new forms of prejudice and discrimination about gay psycho-sexual life styles (Watney 1987).

HIV and AIDS also have major implications for patterns of heterosexual activity. It remains to be seen whether or not high levels of infection will develop among heterosexuals in Britain, but in so far as all those who are sexually active are at potential risk, the behavioural and attitudinal consequences are enormous. This fear of HIV has tremendous psychological as well as physiological potential for threatening marriages. It is likely to create anxiety, concern and mistrust between spouses, forcing them to come to terms with issues of monogamy and infidelity. It will engender huge pressures within relationships where a spouse becomes infected, perhaps going on to become sick with AIDS. One survey (Sanders 1983, 1985) suggests that approximately a third of married men and a quarter of married women have had extramarital sexual relationships; whereas a more recent study (Lawson 1988) found that in a group including first and second marriages, some 73 per cent of respondents reported experience of extramarital sexual relations. So the potential consequences of these issues are very wide. Again, there are major implications for the climate of opinion, norms and values surrounding sexual relationships both inside and outside marriage and there is no doubt that both researchers and practitioners will need to understand these more fully in the future.

HEALTH

A recent comprehensive review, drawing on a range of epidemiological studies, posits a close relationship between health and marital status (Macintyre 1985). Taking into account standardized mortality rates, as well as chronic and acute illness episodes, it is clear that the general health of those who are married is better than that of their single, widowed, divorced or separated counterparts. Significantly, these differences are greater for men than for women. The implication of this data is that 'Marriage is more protective of good health for men than it is for women – or, alternatively, that being single, divorced or widowed is worse, compared to marriage, for men than it is for women' (Macintyre 1985:18). This is further supported by Lynch's (1977) review of a variety of North American material which suggests that life style is an important factor in determining dramatic health differences between the married and the non-married. Death rates for heart disease, the leading cause of death in men, are twice as high among divorced as single men. Differences in other conditions, such as cancer of the respiratory and digestive systems, stroke, cirrhosis of the liver and pneumonia are between two and six times higher among divorced men that their married counterparts. There are also dramatic differences between the married and the divorced in deaths by suicide, homicide and motor vehicle accident. In health terms therefore it would seem that husbands have more to lose than their wives by the ending of a marriage.

Eichenbaum and Orbach (1984) have articulated this paradox from a psychological perspective; they show how men's *dependency* needs are both more hidden in our culture, but ironically more likely to be met. For men, dependence on mother is replaced by dependence on wife; for women however there is no such reciprocal relationship, but only psychological crises of various kinds, which become labelled as problems of dependency.

It is of course in the area of mental health where important differences show up in male–female experiences of marriage. Levels of psycho-social illness are at their highest for young mothers at home with their children, especially when the women also lack a confidante or close relationship outside of the marriage, such as with a friend or mother (Brown and Harris 1978). It is clear from this that the reverse side of the marriage relationship, which protects and bolsters the psycho-social well-being of men, is the one which impoverishes that of women. To that extent the marital world may become a psychic prison, rather than a haven; a place more likely to destroy than nurture. This is shown most graphically of all in studies of wife abuse (Dobash and Dobash 1980).

MARRIAGE OR COHABITATION?

As we have seen, there has been a recent decline in the absolute number of marriages occurring in Britain. In 1971 459,000 marriages took place, compared with 389,000 in 1983 (CSO 1985:36). These figures of course are related to the age and marital status structure of the population at a given time and reflect the numbers that are eligible for marriage. However, they also imply a real decline, mainly accounted for by the falling rate of first marriage (CSO 1985:37); this involves especially a reduction in the rates of teenage marriage.

The increase in the practice of cohabitation has been linked to these trends, with discussion centring around whether or not cohabitation should be seen as a 'trial period' leading up to marriage, or as a substitute for it. The practice of cohabitation is likely to have contributed to the general increase in age at marriage. We know that 7 per cent of British women aged 20 to 24 were cohabiting in 1981–2. Likewise about one quarter of first marriages may be expected to be preceded by the partners living together. Cohabitation prior to second marriage is much more common and is now found in about two-thirds of cases (Clark 1987:113).

How should such figures be interpreted? We must remember that informal unions of a quasi-marital nature are known to exist in the historical record. Similarly, in Scotland marriage by *habit and repute*, in which a couple who are free to marry may live together and be treated as if legally married, has existed since the sixteenth century (Haldane 1982:3). Although the research evidence is limited, at least one study of the meaning of contemporary cohabitation suggests a wide range of cohabiting partnerships. These include couples living together as an agreed prelude to marriage; stable relationships which have evolved from an earlier, more temporary relationship or shared accommodation; and cohabiting partnerships with little expectation of permanence (Burgoyne 1985). To these we should also add heterosexual, gay and lesbian relationships which are deliberately defined in contradistinction to the institution and relationship of marriage.

Burgoyne's study suggests that increasing cohabitation among young people may be associated with higher levels of parental divorce, creating among their offspring a scepticism or caution about getting married. As some of these children of divorced parents remarked, marriage may not be all it is 'cracked up' to be (1985:10). In this sense, cohabitation as either trial marriage or as a substitute for it would imply some underlying instrumental rationality in the construction of partnerships. This is of course true of the rhetorics of cohabitation: that it does not take for granted the implicit rules of the culture, and to that extent provides an opportunity for more satisfying and 'equal' relationships. But as Burgoyne shows, under closer examination, 'neither participants or observers find that such partnerships differ very greatly from those of "ordinary" or "normal" married couples' (1985:17). This was true in a variety of areas, including financial management, the domestic division of labour and questions of sexual fidelity. It was particularly marked in relation to having children, and Burgoyne reports that among her respondents 'there was little enthusiasm for the idea of having or bringing up children outside of marriage even though they recognised that illegitimacy did not carry the same stigma as it had done in the past' (1985:20). This says a good deal about the ways in which 'settling down', 'getting married' and 'having children' still tend to be conflated in our culture, and in particular the strong influence which these notions have on young people. It is for this reason that Mansfield (1985) prefers to regard high levels of cohabitation as a new and final phase of courtship, rather than signalling any fundamental change in patterns of couple formation.

Of course, it is also important to recognize the importance of gender differences in some of these processes. Young women are thought to devote more of their time than young men to the activity of finding, maintaining and discussing their relationships with potential partners (McRobbie 1978; Brake 1980); and they are more likely to be preoccupied by the relationship itself (Sarsby 1983). The newlywed women studied by Mansfield (1985) also tended to describe themselves as more eager to get married than their husbands. By contrast, some of Burgoyne's cohabiting working-class men described with some pleasure their achievement in having avoided the conventional route into marriage (Burgoyne 1985).

The majority of couples still live in the parental home until the time of their first marriage (Kiernan 1985), so that getting married may be about escaping one way of life, as well as creating another. We do not know what proportion of men and women marry their first 'serious' partner, though most of the young women interviewed by Mansfield indicated that they had married the first or second person with whom they had a serious relationship (Mansfield 1985). The autonomy and adult status which getting married bestows could therefore be seen as a trade-off against the possibility of greater freedoms and other relationships. This tension, according to Askham (1984), forms the main contradiction in all marriages: the conflict between stability and identity. Marriage *can* provide both, but for either husband or wife these competing tendencies are unlikely to rest in a state of satisfying equilibrium. The evidence reviewed here however does not suggest that unmarried cohabitation, rather than legal marriage, has produced a more satisfactory resolution of the problem.

STARTING A FAMILY

Germaine Greer (1985) in her polemical work on the declining fertility of the Western nations has described our culture as child-hating, rather than child-centred. In terms of both fertility rates and patterns of child rearing, this argument bears examination; yet it remains the case that some 90 per cent of couples have children, albeit in fewer numbers than a century ago and in the context of greater life expectancy and a steady ageing of the population as a whole. Viewed from the life course perspective therefore, the experience of bearing babies and rearing small children now occupies a fairly restricted number of years for most couples.

A recent review by Busfield (1987) shows how these changing demographic patterns have been embellished by particular ideological connotations. There has been for example a growing interest, on the part of both academic social scientists and popular commentators, in aspects of *parenting*. The term itself reflects the common tendency to assume an increasingly egalitarian set of relationships in marriages which are based on notions of partnership. As we have already shown, such concepts, of 'companionate marriages' and 'symmetrical families' should be treated with caution. As Busfield points out, these terms are themselves complex social constructions, which reflect the political and policy concerns of their period, as well as the theoretical fashions of the social sciences (1987:68). We should therefore beware of using them uncritically, not least because they may serve to mask important gender differences in the experience of being a mother or a father.

Nevertheless, it would appear that within our culture *starting a family* is seen as a fundamental goal for many married couples, an achievement which finally sets the seal on their marital status. Indeed, a number of studies (Busfield and Paddon 1977) have shown the close interconnections of marriage expectations and the desire to have children: 'Just you and me, and baby makes three', as the song so charmingly puts it. But the converse has also applied; so that Macintyre found in her study of unmarried pregnancy that a woman who did not intend to marry was assumed by medical staff to want her pregnancy terminated (Macintyre 1976). This has to be understood in the context of a society which places great value on the emotional rewards of parenthood, particularly for women, and where to be married and to have a family is to place one's mark on future generations (Busfield 1974).

EMPLOYMENT AND UNEMPLOYMENT

For many years it was a common assumption in sociology that the industrial revolution had produced a radical separation between home and workplace. Whereas in the agrarian past, the household had been the site and unit of production, with the development of industrial processes the family unit itself became more and more one of *consumption*. This was linked to certain ideologies of the industrial world. During the Victorian period towns and cities, with their factories and concentrations of population, were portrayed as dark, threatening places. By contrast, the domestic world of home and family was seen as a place of safety or retreat, and in particular a safe haven for women and children who were confined within it. So powerful were these images that they were often idealized by families lower down the social scale, even those in which, from economic necessity, the female members were forced out into paid employment. It is not difficult to see how ideas of this kind served to mould the experience of married women in the twentieth century. Within new, idealized 'companionate' marriages they should remain at home as nurturers and carers, carefully maintaining the 'haven in a heartless world' (Lasch 1977) into which the husband could retreat at the end of the day. Taking such ideologies largely for granted, sociology then went on to separate the world into 'public' and 'private' domains and to see these two areas of social life as increasingly dichotomous and mutually exclusive.

It has largely been the task of feminism to deconstruct the work/family nexus, by highlighting the *continuities* which still exist between the worlds of paid and unpaid work and especially the ways in which they affect women. We have already referred to this in terms of differing expectations which men and women have of the relationship between marriage and work. It is particularly revealed by the ways in which many women are subtly *incorporated* (Callan and Ardener 1984) as unpaid collaborators in their husbands' paid employment. While occupations such as the ministry and general practice, along with self-employment in small businesses have been obvious examples of this (Finch 1983), it is notable that a number of other more traditional male occupations, such as mining, fishing or long-distance lorry driving also created very specific implications for wives (Dennis et al. 1959; Tunstall 1962; Hollowell 1968). More recently this has been shown in the case of a new 'extreme' occupation, employment in the offshore oil industry, in which the workers alternate between fixed and continuous periods of work on the rig or platform, juxtaposed with similar stretches of time at home (Clark and Taylor 1988). Women married to workers in a variety of occupations may therefore find themselves constrained by aspects of their husbands' public role, or expectations which attach to it. They may be unpaid secretaries, message-takers or errand runners; they may be limited in their own careers by their husbands' irregular working hours or employment patterns.

To an extent though, *all* wives are 'married to the job', as Finch (1983) puts it. Indeed, married women are likely to take responsibility for a mix of unpaid domestic work, along with remunerated employment outside the home. There has been a dramatic increase in women's involvement in the labour market over the past 30 years. It is now only mothers of children aged under five years who are significantly underrepresented in the ranks of paid labour. But as with their activities in the home, so too in the labour market, women's work is likely to follow particular gender patterns; being of lower status, with an emphasis on caring and nurturing roles, such as teacher, nurse or domestic worker. Barrett and McIntosh (1982) attribute this to the all-pervading *familism* of the contemporary world, arguing that images of the family are not in decline, but persist as powerful influences upon the way we construct male and female identities in more public settings, such as the labour market, in education or in social policy. High levels of female paid employment should not be regarded therefore as the key to automatic sexual equality.

This is brought out in even more marked cases where wives are in paid employment but their husbands are not. Morris's (1985) study of redundant steelworkers has shown that even when wives become the sole breadwinners, notions about male authority in the household still continue and men are unlikely to become more involved in domestic activity. Conversely, breadwinning wives may be reluctant to give up aspects of personal control and authority within the household arrangements. As Burgoyne has put it: 'There is very little evidence that high levels of male unemployment and, in some areas, increased part-time job opportunities for women, are encouraging role 'swaps' or alterations in traditional domestic divisions of labour' (1987:54).

CLASS AND CULTURE

As we shall see again in part 4, the dimension of social class has been of considerable interest to sociologists studying family life in Britain. For a time this was mainly directed at families in the working class, as in a number of classic studies carried out in the East End of London, in Northern industrial communities and among traditional occupations, such as fishermen and miners. Much of this discussion centred around the extent to which the working-class extended family was breaking down and being replaced by smaller, more isolated nuclear families, composed solely of mother, father and their offspring. In the case of Young and Willmott's (1957) famous inquiry into migration from the East End to the Essex suburbs, the rise of the nuclear family was also linked to new patterns of working-class consumption and leisure, along with emerging values concerning the centrality of the home and the domestic world.

This was the period when Britain had 'never had it so good'; an era which saw a growing trend towards home ownership and local authority housing provision, allowing a generation of newly-weds to establish themselves from the outset in homes of their own, apart from their parents. It was also an era of political conservatism, when during the 1950s three successive Conservative governments were returned to office. Such phenomena posed complex analytical problems at the time for sociologists of the left. A new theory of change in the working class began to emerge, that of *embourgeoisement*. With increased affluence, the rise of the new blue-collar occupations and increasing geographical mobility, came changes in working-class life styles and value systems. One aspect of this was a growing emphasis upon 'privatized' domestic spending and shared leisure time between spouses, along with their correlates – the erosion of workplace solidarity, of union membership, of work-related leisure groups and, above all, a preference for Tory rather than Labour policies (Goldthorpe et al. 1969).

These structural changes were also seen to have implications for the marital relationship. Material investments in home and household were mirrored by emotional commitments to new-style conjugal roles, where couples spent more time together and engaged in self-conscious planning of family futures – decisions about when to have children, move to a larger house, change job and so on. For some this was seen as the working class inexorably moving forward to enjoy the material and psychological benefits previously limited to those higher up the pecking order. Young and Willmott (1975) referred to this as a process of 'stratified diffusion', wherein the domestic goods and services of 'the few' in one generation were accessible to 'the many' in the next.

There is of course much to be criticized in such explanations. Once again we are made acutely aware of the tendency for academic social commentators to reinforce and reflect, rather than deconstruct, the prevailing values and assumptions of their time. As we can now see from the vantage point of the late 1980s, social class is still a major source of division within our society. And class inequalities continue to manifest themselves in various aspects of family life, such as fertility, health and illness patterns, housing and divorce rates. In particular we have seen the emergence of an under-class characterized by chronic social problems, which is increasingly distanced from the material and psychological world of what has been referred to as 'comfortable Britain'. Such examples should alert us, as researchers and practitioners, to the dangers of viewing the world solely from the vantage point of our own personal or professional experience, or through the filters of our own preferred ideologies. The continuing presence of coherent class differences within our society poses major problems for any analysis of contemporary marriage, and it would be a great mistake to generalize uncritically from present-day middle-class marriages to those of other classes, now or in the future.

2.3 Marital Tensions

It should be clear, even from this broad-brushstroke review, that understanding marriage in our society depends heavily upon an ability to recognize the interconnectedness of both structural and personal factors. Social research has the tools to deconstruct the marital world, exposing the underpinnings of such factors as gender, class, age or employment. But these alone give us only a partial account; emphasizing the externalities, they often ignore internal realities, such as issues of process and meaning within marriage and the ways in which these may be influenced by wider cultural, political and ideological agendas. Nowhere is the need to bridge this gap more evident than in the explanation of marital problems. In this section we shall therefore explore some of the ways in which marital problems are socially and personally constructed and relate these to what is known about trends in marriage and divorce.

THE SOCIAL CONSTRUCTION OF MARITAL PROBLEMS

The propensity to define certain aspects of the institution and the relationship called marriage as *problematic* should be seen as a product of specific cultural and historical circumstances. 'Problems' occur in marriage not merely because they constitute some aspect of the subjective experience of spouses, but also because they have been identified by other interest groups who define their significance in particular ways. This may seem a perverse position to adopt; surely the experience of 'unhappiness' in a marriage is not new, and there have 'always' been 'good' and 'bad' marriages? We would not dispute this, and indeed the historical record gives us some insight into the varying textures of marriages in former times, albeit more those of the upper than the lower classes (Trumbach 1978). But the desire precisely to define the nature of marital problems, to list and codify, to measure and map and above all else to attempt to develop specific services to help those in 'distress', these are all historically fairly recent phenomena. They tell us something about how expectations of marriage have changed since the late-Victorian period and how these changes have been in turn linked to the development of new ideologies about marriage. It is important to keep this in mind when referring to some apparent category of phenomena called 'marital problems', not least because marriage in our culture, and the complex family and kinship arrangements which surround it, continue to be invested with a set of natural and taken-for-granted meanings which render their analysis either unnecessary or impossible. With marital, as with other social problems, we are therefore prudent continually to keep in mind the sceptical question, 'says who?'

Brannen and Collard (1982) in seeking to locate within a wider social context their empirical findings about help-seeking in marriage, identify three related spheres of public discussion around marriage and divorce. These discussions, though involving conflicting and differing values, contribute to a *discourse* on marriage and its problems which is historically specific. Firstly, Brannen and Collard identify the positions adopted by a number of interconnected power elites: churches, politicians and the law. These, whether reformist or conservative in character, tend to be rooted in an acceptance of existing norms and values surrounding marriage, usually seeing them as under threat in some way. Debates within the women's movement however, the second of the spheres, are explicitly committed to the critique of the existing structural and cultural arrangements affecting marriage. The third group, and one to which we shall devote considerable space in part 4, is the growing body of 'human service' practitioners who increasingly see 'marital problems' as a legitimate area for professional concern and intervention. Each of the three contributes to a climate in which the internal and external aspects of marriage, its relational and institutional dimensions, become legitimate material for public debate and social action. This may lead to contradictions and conflicts, such as when one group's problem is another's solution. For example, conservative voices may argue that the strains placed upon marriage emanate from the increased numbers of women in the labour market. Feminists however may take the view that the achievement of women's equal participation in the labour market with men is merely the prerequisite for more egalitarian domestic arrangements between men and women, whether married or not. Practitioners, for their part may agree there are external pressures on marriage (though how they are defined and where they come from may be of less concern) and that these necessarily require the intervention of skilled helpers if they are to be properly 'dealt with' and resolved. By these criteria, 'marital problems' will come in very different guises. Perhaps all that the different interest groups have in common is a willingness to 'problematize' the phenomenon of marriage. For some this will be through appeals to natural justice, traditional values or some form of social morality; for others it will turn around issues of power, ideology and history; for a further group it may find expression in a litany of personal ills, traumas and crises affecting couples in the intimate world of the marriage relationship.

Writing more explicitly for a social work audience, James and Wilson (1986) offer a chapter on 'Problems in marital relationships'; their terminology is interesting, at once implying that these are problems more narrowly relational than *marital*, in the sense of a phenomenon which has both personal and societal dimensions. However the authors do acknowledge the problems of bringing together research data, which in the main 'looks at marriage from the outside' and understandings which are concerned with 'the reality of marriages from the inside' (1986:29). They point out that rates of divorce in a society are poor indicators of levels of marital unhappiness, since some marriages which exhibit high levels of conflict and difficulties are not at all likely to end in divorce. We would add to this that divorce rates are to some extent an artefact of divorce legislation. When they are in the ascendant they should not necessarily be seen as an indicator of mounting unhappiness within marriage, but perhaps as evidence of the growing congruence between levels of unhappiness and the ability to end a marriage as a result of more liberal divorce laws. To that extent recent decades may have served only to make visible levels of marital unhappiness which have existed for some time, but were not open to the public gaze.

David Morgan (1985), in an interesting chapter on the 'medicalisation of marriage' argues that the assumption of some class of problems called 'marital problems' is evidence of the application of a *medical model* to the understanding of marriage. Marital problems from this perspective are therefore classifiable, reduceable and treatable. They will be perceived as 'problems to do with the complex pattern of emotional, interpersonal and sexual relationships that constitute marriage' (1985:35). They may also be seen as the underlying 'cause' of a wide range of other social issues: delinquency, homelessness or teenage pregnancy. It flows from this model that these wider problems could be ameliorated by seeking to 'cure' the underlying cause, a task for therapeutic intervention. Within this approach to marital problems there has perhaps been a tendency to give particular emphasis to *sexual* problems, issues which are defined in such terms as 'dysfunctions' or 'abnormalities'. Drawing on Foucault's (1979) work on the history of sexuality, Morgan reminds us that the process of disengagement in recent decades from a variety of legal, moral and religious taboos, which is often described as one of sexual liberation, has in fact given way to other forms of social control. These are the 'thou shalts' of medical, therapeutic and counselling ideologies which seek to determine the range and content of 'meaningful' or 'fulfilling' sexual relations. By such means it may be that the sex manual replaces the abominations of Leviticus as a key determinant of sexual mores, in a discourse where sexual and marital satisfactions become inextricably linked.

Finally, we note an apparent paradox in the debate about marital problems. We saw in earlier sections when exploring issues of gender, health, employment and child-bearing that it was possible to identify a number of areas in which 'marriages', more accurately *husbands* or *wives*, may experience difficulties and unhappiness at particular times, usually in relation to some aspect of their place in the life course. We have an increasingly clear understanding of how these difficulties can occur, of the personal and structural factors which promote them and of their place within the contemporary discourse on marriage. Paradoxically, we have very little insight into sources of satisfaction in marital relationships, or indeed why it is that even now approximately two-thirds of marriages taking place will endure until the death of one or other of the partners. All the evidence suggests that increased longevity and the particular range of material and emotional pressures which now surround marriage would make lifelong matrimony a steadily more difficult achievement. Yet it remains both the goal and the reality for the large majority of those who marry; and that is certainly a subject which merits further research.

PERSONAL ACCOUNTS OF MARRIAGE DISSOLUTION

The sociological literature of recent years has produced a number of accounts of marriage dissolution, gathered for slightly differing research purposes. These provide detailed examples of the ways in which men and women describe their own personal experience of marital difficulties and the range of meanings which are attributed to them. They also provide the basis for broader generalizations about problems and expectations within marriage, which have theoretical and heuristic value. In this section we shall explore the range of these accounts and consider their place within the context of a wider public debate about marriage and divorce. First of all however it is important to say something of the way in which we regard such data, since they raise a number of problems of methodology and interpretation.

Although a great deal has changed within the last few decades, sociological research in general has not been noted for its concern to record the things that people say, or indeed to place individuals, families or groups at the centre of its research preoccupations. Sociology has had a long history of examining other kinds of data: trends, frequencies, indices, in which to a large extent the personal actions, motives and beliefs of individuals are obscured. It is welcome therefore to see the growing acceptance of an approach to sociological research which puts the human actor centre stage and allows her or his voice to be heard. We shall say a good deal more about this process, as it affects marriage research, in part 4. One of its effects is that we are now able to identify in the literature a number of studies in which personal accounts of marriage and its problems are subjected to sociological analysis. In exploring them here we should make clear that we see these accounts not as 'the facts' about what is happening in a particular group of marriages; they should not therefore be used to generate inferences about trends within marriage in general. Nor should they even be regarded as the 'true' experiences of those involved, enabling us categorically to explain the particular details of their situation. Rather they provide us with 'texts' from which we should seek to 'read off' an understanding of marriage within our culture. They present us with a range of experiences, they offer insights into how these are encountered differently by men and women, they show us that even the innermost feelings of intimate relationships may be signposted or coloured by far wider social agendas and processes.

In an early ethnographic study of divorce, in which Hart (1976) explored the experiences of members of a Midlands club for the divorced and separated, a distinction was drawn between two forms of marital dissolution. Hart contrasted 'active' and 'passive' roles in the process of separation, according to the manner in which the marriage ended. Thus those spouses who deserted, or forced their partner to leave were classified as active, whereas those who were forced out or abandoned could be seen as passive. This now seems a highly simplistic method of categorizing styles of marital dissolution, since it relies solely on the apparently 'visible' explanation, to wit that of only one of the spouses to the marriage. It is indicative, in a sense, of the sociologist's desire to construct some kind of order or pattern out of the range of personal experience; whereas what is more important is the person's *interpretation* of what took place, rather than any apparently objective description of it. As we shall show in parts 4 and 5 this 'account' is something which should arise out of the collaborative efforts of both researcher and 'subject'; it should not remain the product merely of the researcher's analysis.

Burgoyne and Clark (1984), taking a lead from Hart, were able to develop a more sensitive approach to the problem, albeit one which still relied on just one partner's account of the process. They too distinguish between 'active' and 'passive' roles in the ending of a marriage, but base these on the person's subjective definition of the situation. So that, for example, the wife who tolerates her husband's continued infidelities over a long period of time but who finally insists that he leaves the matrimonial home, is regarded as 'active' rather than passive; particularly as the explanation of these events may include a growing sense of empowerment on the part of the wife, finally freeing her to take some action. As Burgoyne and Clark show in a series of detailed case examples, it is difficult and unhelpful to seek to attribute simplistic labels as to the reasons for marriage dissolution. In that sense the notion of matrimonial causes, which were until recently enshrined in law, and which still bulk large in popular consciousness, does considerable violence to the complexity of the situation as experienced. It is a partial story indeed to explain the ending of a marriage by 'mental cruelty', 'infidelity', 'unreasonable behaviour' or whatever. Burgoyne and Clark however are less interested in such classifications for their own sake than for the light they may shed on 'the factors which lead the separated and divorced person into new relationships, including cohabitation and remarriage' (1984:55); this is something to which we shall return later.

Whereas Burgoyne and Clark's (1984) work was conducted with a study group which had not in general been exposed to social work and counselling interventions, Brannen and Collard (1982) studied a number of couples who had experience of counselling or therapy. The authors contend that 'the ways in which the partners in the marriage accommodated (or failed to accommodate) to marriage troubles are related to the processes by which they constructed accounts and made attributions of their problems' (1982:47). In other words the 'experience' of marital problems is the product of a process in which meaning is given to certain thoughts, feelings, circumstances or events. For Brannen and Collard however this process must be seen within the context of 'a relationship that is historically embedded in a system of power which significantly discriminates against women' and in which 'the inequality between husbands and wives is largely stabilized by the deference of one partner (the wife) to the other (the husband)' (1982:49). In this study it was most common for partners to apportion blame to each other for the problems in the marriage; there was little mutual agreement or mutual apportionment. These marriages had 'guilty' and 'innocent' parties, in which wives were usually more willing than their husbands to 'accept' the blame for what had gone wrong. The two most problematic areas within the marriages were 'sexual activity, on the one hand and communication and demonstrativeness on the other' (1982:51). In the latter context it is significant that wives, rather than husbands, were the ones who complained about their spouses' lack of communication and demonstrativeness.

These studies all show that the circumstances which accompany the dissolution of a marriage are potentially very complex; they are therefore difficult to recover for the sociological record. It is important to remember that this is a significant process in its own right; to render an account to the sociological researcher is to engage in the task of giving meaning to something, perhaps some experience that has not been considered in that way before. As we shall see in part 4, this raises a number of methodological problems which are common to both researchers and therapists. It means that we should read personal accounts of marital problems or marriage dissolution with a great deal of caution. When carefully collected and analysed however- er, they provide a very important opportunity to enter into the private dimensions of a world which is most usually presented to us in terms of its public, structural implications.

MASS DIVORCE

The most visible public outcome of marital unhappiness in our society today is of course mass divorce. There has been a dramatic rise in the number of divorces in the United Kingdom since the early 1960s, with figures increasing from 27,000 in 1961, to 80,000 a decade later, to 162,000 in 1983. In this latter year nearly 50 per cent of divorces occurred before the couples' tenth wedding anniversary and 20 per cent took place before five years of marriage; 20 per cent of these divorces involved at least one previously divorced partner (CSO 1985:39). About seven divorces in ten involve children under the age of 16.

Within these broad patterns there are a number of significant regional and cultural differences. At ten per thousand, divorce rates in Scotland are some 20 per cent lower than in England and Wales. There is also a clear relationship between social class and divorce; using husbands' occupation as the measure, and with the exception of social class III non-manual, divorce rates decline steadily as the ladder of social class is ascended. Data gathered by Haskey for England and Wales in 1979 shows a rate of divorce of seven per thousand in the professional class, rising to 30 per thousand among unskilled manual workers (Haskey 1984:12). Perhaps most striking of all, Haskey discovered a divorce rate of 34 per thousand among unemployed men of all classes. Once again, we can see from these patterns ways in which the 'private trouble' of divorce, an experience which is frequently perceived as the unique personal trauma of those involved, has its public dimensions and is subject to the influence of wider structural factors.

There is some dispute as to whether increasing rates of divorce in the twentieth century should be seen as the cause or the effect of more liberal divorce laws. Richards (1982) for example argues that changes in the law occur in the wake of deeper changes within couples' propensity to divorce. It does seem clear however that taken together there has been a progressive *deregulation* of laws relating to marriage and divorce. Married couples and family members in general have thus moved from a situation in which the constitution of the family unit and the legal relationships of its members were strictly defined and controlled, to one in which a much wider range of family relationships can be accommodated. As Glendon puts it: 'The change is characterised by progressive withdrawal of legal regulation of marriage formation, dissolution and the conduct of married life, on the one hand, and by increased regulation of the economic and child-related consequences of formal or informal cohabitation on the other' (Glendon 1977:321). Matrimonial law has, in short, become less rule-bound and more discretionary.

We are not so much concerned here with the detailed explication of these trends, which have been explored at length by others (Burgoyne, Ormrod and Richards 1987), than with their more general implications for marriage as both institution and relationship. One consequence is that the ending of a marriage by divorce can no longer be regarded as something 'out there', which affects others, but not ourselves. Divorce is no longer the preserve of movie stars and aristocrats, but touches most of us, either directly or indirectly. In family settings and in the workplace, as well as in wider networks of neighbours, friends and kin, it has become commonplace to observe at first hand the personal, material and legal implications which may flow from the experience of marriage break-up and divorce. This has led to a great deal of divorce commentary, from journalists and broadcasters, from churchmen and moralists and from representatives of the caring professions. Divorce has been transformed from a subject which was hedged about with embarrassment to one which excites continuing public interest and is accompanied by a voluminous 'self-help' literature. It is a regular feature of television dramas and soap operas, it is portrayed in children's books and is frequently the subject of television and radio documentary. In certain social groups it appears more normative than lifelong matrimony.

It is far less clear however what bearing this has on individual marriages and on the ways in which husbands and wives hold expectations of marriage and partnership. Most young people still appear to want to get married and most of those who marry apparently expect to remain so. Yet to acknowledge the phenomenon of mass divorce is to recognize the possibility that circumstances may not turn out according to expectations, that conflicts and tensions may occur and that these may be so great as to make remaining in the marital relationship impossible. Despite its increased incidence, divorce continues to bring personal pain, guilt and a sense of failure at having fallen short of the ideal. It can have adverse effects on the health of those involved, particularly men. It can lead to a variety of conflicts between the parties: over property, custody, access and maintenance arrangements. When considering such issues it is important to keep in mind that divorce is less a question of status, and more one of process; that is to say that the experience of divorce will involve a number of personal, emotional, material, economic and legal transitions (Burgoyne, Ormrod and Richards 1987). These may be coterminous, or quite separate in time. For example, the legal ending of a marriage may take place long after the most acute experiences of emotional trauma have passed; a new partnership may be well established before all the financial and material aspects of the divorce are finalized, and so on. Divorce must be seen therefore in the context of the life course, as a process which may coexist with other concerns and commitments: career aspirations, buying a house, raising children. In divorce, as in marriage, these various concerns may not be compatible with one another; the interests of parents and children may appear to be polarized or in conflict; the demands of the employer may continue to ignore the pressures of domestic life; the financial sequelae of divorce may erode access to housing and consumer durables. All of these factors have the capacity to become enmeshed in a complex web which is difficult to sustain for the person and which poses huge interpretive problems for the researcher or counsellor. The evidence suggests that one way in which divorced men and women believe these tensions can be neutralized or resolved is by re-entering, sooner or later, into the state of wedlock.

2.4 Hope versus Experience?

One marriage in three taking place in our society is a remarriage for one or other of the partners. The large majority of those who remarry do so after divorce, rather than the death of a spouse. We have entered a social context where for the first time there is divorce *and* remarriage on a mass scale. This 'triumph of hope over experience', Doctor Johnson's description of remarriage, has therefore become a significant component in the totality of marital relationships in our society. Getting married for a second, or even subsequent, time can no longer be seen as an experience on the margins of family life; it is both commonplace and increasingly regarded as a legitimate attempt to find personal happiness after the difficulties associated with the break-up of an earlier marriage. To speak in these terms is of course to acknowledge the major cultural shift which has taken place in public perceptions of marriage; this can be expressed as a growing preoccupation with its *relational* character, at the expense of its institutional dimensions. Mass remarriage seems only to be possible in a society which is less concerned with marriage as a legal, moral and religious edifice and more attentive to its place within the spectrum of adult personal relationships.

The processes of getting married, divorcing and marrying again are best seen as a series of events concentrated for many adults within a fairly narrow band of the life course. General Household Survey data combined for 1981–2 have shown that over a half of women who separated in 1970–74 at ages below 35 had remarried within six years. Little is known about the personal and psychological consequences of concentrating these major life events within a relatively narrow time band. It is known however, that rates of remarriage are three to four times higher for men than women. The risk of re-divorce is also gender specific; divorced men who remarry are more than one and a half times as likely to divorce as single men of the same age marrying for the first time, while for divorced women the chance is twice that of their first-married counterparts (CSO 1985:38).

Indeed, remarriage provides an interesting example of what is referred to in the North American literature as marital *heterogamy*, the tendency for men and women to choose marriage partners who are unlike themselves in terms of age, previous marital status, educational background and so on. Couples marrying for the first time tend to be very similar in broad demographic terms. Most women marry men about two years older than themselves and most of these marriages occur among couples in their early to mid-twenties. Such couples are likely to share similar cultural and generation-specific expectations about marriage, about having children and about domestic life in general. By contrast remarrying couples are more diverse. As one of us has shown in an earlier paper, taking into account the combinations of previous marital and parental status, there are some 55 pathways to remarriage (Clark 1982). In England and Wales the most common form of remarriage is that occurring between two divorced partners; these account for almost a third of all remarriages. In Scotland the most frequent form is that between the divorced man and the spinster. However about a half of all remarriages throughout Britain involve one partner who is marrying for the *first* time. In addition, the age at which remarriage takes place and the relative ages of the spouses are significant factors. The age range of both male and female remarrying divorcees is much wider than that of their first-married counterparts. While the average age gap between remarrying divorcees in England and Wales is only three years, remarriages involving one divorced and one previously unmarried partner often involve a considerably larger age gap; and in the case of bachelors marrying divorced women the 'normal' pattern of the man as the elder partner is often reversed (OPCS Monitor 1984). These men, of course, may also become 'instant' parents to their wives' children by a previous marriage. Statistics relating to those who divorced in England and Wales in 1982 suggest that remarriages in which only *one* partner has been married before are more likely to end in divorce than those in which *both* are remarrying. Amongst this group of 'mixed' remarriages there is some slight evidence that a wider age gap between the spouses increases vulnerability to divorce.

Despite this evidence of plurality, commentators still rather arbitrarily distinguish between 'marriage' and 'remarriage' as if they can be neatly characterized as separate social phenomena. Our interest here, by contrast, is in the continuities which exist between the two and the ways in which marriage and remarriage constitute important processes in the life course. Ironically, it is often through careful attention to questions of *remarriage* that we can better understand marriage itself.

EMOTIONAL AND MATERIAL LEGACIES

Burgoyne and Clark (1984) in their study of remarried couples in Sheffield, found that the men and women they interviewed had carried a complex legacy of the past into their new relationships. The extent to which individual spouses or couples were able to acknowledge this legacy varied a great deal, but it seemed to have two distinct dimensions. The authors therefore distinguish between legacies from the past which are essentially *emotional* in character and those which are predominantly *material*. These two strands clearly have the capacity to intermesh in subtle ways which make them difficult to disentangle; they may appear as a seamless web to those involved, making it impossible to separate out personal, psychological issues from the more concrete realities, of property, possessions and financial settlements.

For the sociologist to acknowledge the existence of an emotional legacy of the past raises the question once again of how accounts of personal life are constructed in the course of the research interview. This takes us into the exploration of aspects of human experience which are to some degree bound up with a sense of identity and personal worth. To this extent they tell us something about the person's view of the world, and in this they may point to wider ideological and cultural representations of marriage, divorce and remarriage in society. This is revealed most clearly in the link between how the ending of the previous marriage is related to the beginning of the new relationship. We saw earlier that despite well-ventilated rhetorics about the high incidence of marriages which end by the 'mutual agreement' of the parties, the research evidence still points to a situation in which marriage break-up is typically experienced as the 'fault' of one or other spouse.

In the Sheffield study those who described themselves as relatively 'active' in the ending of their previous marriage tended to explain their experience in broadly similar terms. These men and women described a sense of growing ennui in the marriage relationship, which was increasingly experienced as unsatisfying, lacking in personal rewards and the source of a variety of frustrations. These respondents described a process of 'drifting' in the marriage, or one in which the partners 'grew apart'. It is interesting to note that these explanations, which now seem so commonplace within our culture, are probably of very recent origin; they certainly reflect the extent to which counselling and therapeutic models of marriage have been internalized within popular understanding. Though the felt experience may have been similar, it is hard to imagine the unhappy spouse of the mid-nineteenth-century marriage using such language to describe it.

These experiences seem in turn to have affected subsequent circumstances and relationships. Individuals in this 'active' group were more likely to seek ways of resolving their dilemmas, usually through new relationships outside marriage. Indeed, they would typically have left the marriage partner in order to begin living with someone else, often with no interval in between. The possibility of happiness with someone else created the opportunity to end an unhappy marriage; this process however was often accompanied by a great deal of personal distress, guilt and self-examination. This sometimes produced bouts of ill health and a variety of psychosomatic symptoms during periods of indecision about whether to stay with the marriage or make the break in order to be with a new spouse.

In contrast to these cases, there were examples of men and women who portrayed their experience of marriage break-up in very different ways, emphasizing the extent to which they felt 'acted against' in the process. For these people, the earlier marriage had often been quite satisfactory, perhaps happy, rewarding and highly valued; they had been content in the marriage while their spouses had not. In some cases the realization of this had come quite suddenly, with little advance warning, when for example they had been told about or discovered the existence of 'another' man or woman. The former spouse's infidelity was therefore the most common explanation for the ending of these marriages. Accordingly the period of ill health or psychological trauma, which seems so often to accompany marriage break-up, had occurred after, rather than before, the separation. There had also been, in contrast to their more 'active' counterparts, a period of living alone prior to establishing a new relationship; this could serve in some cases to provide a kind of 'buffer', an opportunity to reflect on what had happened and perhaps assemble some new priorities for the future.

The need to arrive at some explanation of why the previous marriage had ended seemed to be heightened with the process of starting a new relationship. Respondents in the Sheffield study could be ranked on a broad continuum in their approach to this. Some opted for highly particularistic explanations: they had simply chosen the wrong kind of partner, or someone who would never be able to make a successful marriage for some apparently personal, perhaps pathological reason. Success in the remarriage was therefore merely dependent upon choosing more carefully or insightfully the second time around, but with the continuing sense of luck and chance. Others, while still holding to individualistic explanations of what had happened, pointed to their youth and inexperience at the time of first getting married, and contrasted this with a greater degree of worldliness and wisdom later. Some saw themselves as part of a social trend; they rejected any notion, apparently imputed by the wider society, that to divorce was a sign of personal failure, and argued instead that divorce and remarriage are now common experiences, affecting growing numbers of couples, and to that extent have become 'normal' features of modern life. Between these individualistic and general extremes there was also a group who appeared to have no specific explanation for their experiences; they seemed to have little insight into the personal and social processes they had encountered, and were often unable to satisfy themselves through the construction of some plausible account, even when encouraged to do so in the context of a research interview. In these cases it seemed likely that the emotional legacy of the past had not been adequately worked through, and was to that extent likely to continue to protrude unhelpfully into their present and future relationships.

This interplay between past and present experiences is much more overt in subsequent than in first marriages; for those who remarry there is likely to be a well-developed process of looking back on past difficulties, while at the same time looking forward to the expectation of a better future. Burgoyne and Clark (1984) describe this as the self-conscious pursuit of 'ordinary' family life, the attempt to construct some 'ordinary' set of relationships out of the legacy of the past. In this we may see couples quite consciously, in the remarriage, seeking to establish an 'instant' history and set of traditions, marking key events in the ritual calendar of family life. They may place a particular investment in constructing a joint life style together, a set of values, attitudes, leisure-time pursuits, eating routines, which are uniquely their own, and which reflect their relationship. The pressures to do this may feel particularly great when the ending of a previous marriage is seen as a 'failure', creating increased pressure to succeed the second time.

Such aspirations however are easily frustrated, in particular as a result of the power of the *material* legacy of the past, which may go on intruding into the remarriage over a considerable period of time. In material terms, it is rarely possible for remarried couples to 'forget' the past. They may go on living in the former matrimonial home, with all the household reminders of the previous marriage around them, such as wedding presents, prized possessions, household decorations decided with the former spouse and networks of friends and neighbours which go back to the time of the first marriage. Powerful reminders may occur in their contacts with public institutions and statutory services of various kinds: the courts, lawyers, welfare agencies, social workers, housing and educational services. The interventions of these groups may have a significant and continuing effect on the material circumstances in which the remarriage is constituted. Some couples are likely to experience a disproportionate amount of public control, and this of course will tend to relate to their position within the wider social class and occupational structure.

For those with children, for whom remarriage means the creation of some form of stepfamily, a variety of other legacies will be evident. In these cases the emotional and the material are often inextricably intertwined. For example, there may be a need for continuing contact with the former spouse in order to deal with the practical arrangements of access visits and maintenance payments. Continuing contact may make it difficult to make a 'fresh' start with a new partner; it may be experienced as disruptive to the children, and the access visit may turn into a battleground where the former partners go on playing out the conflicts of their earlier marriage. We do not wish to digress here into a detailed discussion of the broader issue of stepfamilies, but it is worth remembering that for perhaps the majority of remarriages, making a 'fresh' start with a new spouse is also accompanied by the creation of some form of stepfamily, a set of social arrangements which, as Visher and Visher (1979) put it, is always 'born out of loss'.

Paradoxically, to look carefully at remarriage can highlight our levels of understanding and ignorance about marriage more generally. In examining the processes whereby marriage is constituted after divorce, we see writ large many of the assumptions, beliefs and values which underpin the generalities of marriage in society. The same can be true of research on marital problems and break-up: out of the problematic aspects of marital experience can emerge a deeper understanding of what it is that couples seek in a marriage relationship which is now expected to endure for unprecedented periods of time. In this part of the book we have mapped out the major sociological factors which can impact upon and enmesh with the experience of marriage through the life course. In part 3 we begin by picking up these themes as they relate to developmental processes within marriage.

3

Choices and Consequences in Couple Relationships

In part 2 we examined ideologies about marriage and aspects of variations and tensions within marriage, primarily from a sociological perspective. Here, we continue to explore the public and the private, though focusing more on the inner world of marriage, the private reality of men and women in marriage. We shall take note of how the development of identity and individuality is dependent on the nature of the reciprocity between the individual and other persons, as explored by the object relations theorists, for example in the work of Winnicott (1958; 1965a; 1965b). We shall be particularly concerned with the issues of dialogue and encounter in relationships, about how 'I' and 'Thou' are being constantly redefined, however minimally, in interaction and through the dialogue of living (Buber 1958). We shall also explore how these influence responses in counselling and therapy. And we shall discuss how ideas and practices developed particularly in relation to the life of institutions and organizations (Bridger 1981) are relevant to the task of responding effectively to men and women distressed in their marital relationships.

A number of central themes can be identified within the wedlocked state, its potential problems and the work of those involved in attempts to resolve them: the inevitability of the need to make choices and the recognition that relationships such as marriage or those between couples and practitioners, both offer opportunities and carry obligations.

3.1 Opportunities and Obligations

MEN AND WOMEN IN MARRIAGE

The perspective we offer does not try to take into consideration all aspects of the long-term heterosexual relationship called marriage. Instead, we have chosen to look at issues such as opportunities and obligations, conflict and choice, problems and their resolution. These are fundamental to the marital relationship, the tensions to which it may give rise and to ways of responding to these.

Of the basic assumptions which determine our perspective, there are two which we should present here. One is that in general men and women seek and for the most part find a close, long-term, mainly exclusive relationship with a person of the opposite gender. The second is that for most, this relationship is affirmed by the society of which they are part, by their peers and their elders. Most couples seek title to this relationship in public, in the sight and sound of at least their friends and of a person sanctioned to name this relationship and define them as husband and wife. We see this relationship as a search for a person who will respond to one's unmet needs, who will supply what one feels to be missing in oneself. At the same time we regard its institutionalized form as one expression of the need of men and women to have a publicly approved structure and boundary for their long-term relationship. A purpose of this institutionalized dyad, a potential it offers to the constituent individuals, is the possibility of becoming a whole, free person in the continuing relationship with another, who seeks also an acceptable, clear and separate identity: the possibility of finding freedom without isolation, independence without separateness, closeness without engulfment.

On the way to such an achievement, such a having-become, there are stages in development, tasks which have to be undertaken, and these have been summarized (Haldane and McCluskey 1988) as: (1) the mutual care and nurture of each spouse for the other, expressed in the general organization of their life, their work and leisure and in their sexual relationship; (2) the opportunity for, and support in, working through problems, conflicts and difficulties insufficiently resolved at earlier stages of the individuals' lives, within such a mutually caring relationship; (3) the promotion of a fuller realization of the individuals' potential, particularly in personal relationships; (4) the promotion of self-realization, autonomy and independence within the context of bonds of affectionate attachment; (5) the development and maintenance of the capacity to adapt to change (e.g. having children, ageing, adverse external circumstances and in some cases the dissolution of the marriage). Such a process includes the search for joy and happiness, for nurture and comfort, for self-confidence and security, for significance and aliveness; but it is difficult to believe that the majority of those who choose to live together in some form of long-term relationship are not also aware of potential problems and risks. For those who marry, the majority have direct experience of marriage, that of their parents and perhaps extended families. For an increasing proportion, they will have experience of two marriages, perhaps three, as parents divorce and one or both remarry. We have little systematic knowledge of what keeps together the majority who remain married to their first spouse and we cannot assume any widespread agreement about what constitutes a good or satisfactory relationship within marriage. This close attachment entered into by many people in the early part of their lives is not, of course, their first experience of an intimate dyad. The majority who marry have experienced a relationship with a mother, another pair relationship, and with a father and have experienced each of these as one of a threesome. We are not dependent exclusively on professional books and articles for the view that such early relationships, developed more than two decades before the offspring becomes wife or husband, have much influence on marriage. They affect the choice of spouse, the timing of the marriage, the satisfactions and dissatisfactions which will characterize it and how it will end. Both literature and drama respond to and reflect these realities, exploring the ways in which our early lives are unknowingly taken into the adult relationship, which couples enter with such apparent freedom and considered choice.

We see the opportunities and obligations involved in marriage not as an 'either-or' but as a 'both-and', if the relationship is to have a sufficient chance of being maintained while allowing for the development of the personalities of each individual. While the adult relationship makes new demands, it also offers opportunities to work through, to resolve, conflicts and tensions which have their origin in earlier relationships; but there are also tensions which are inevitable in and intrinsic to adult heterosexual relationships, involving a wide range and degree of emotions, as choices are made and new situations arise. Only some of these can be illustrated. Spouses have responsibilities to and for each other, but they need also a sufficient sense of freedom to pursue that which seems authentic and true to their sense of self. Each needs a sense of autonomy, but also to be able to assume a reliance on the other, a necessary degree of interdependence. A stable sense of identity, a necessary foundation for being able to adapt to change, especially if stressful, may conflict with the other's need for flexibility and responsiveness. It is not easy to achieve between husband and wife a mutually acceptable balance between, for example, dominance and submissiveness, strength and weakness, the need for intimacy and the fear of abandonment. Trust in oneself and in the other may be achieved only after much effort, not necessarily aided by open and honest communication. The individual needs to survive as a person within the relationship and not be absorbed into or taken over by the other. The desire for a satisfying sexual relationship contains needs and wishes relating to the self, to the other and to the mutuality of the relationship and not all of these will be congruent at any one time. The sharing of activities and responsibilities may limit the opportunity for privacy and time for oneself; exclusiveness may limit the opportunity for friendships outwith the dyad and an open network of friendships may be experienced as a threat to the dyad.

Such conflicts and tensions exist not only between spouses but also within each individual, tensions which also contain opportunities for resolution. To reach an acceptable balance, individuals need to be able to give each other sufficient psychological space. Conceived of in topographical terms, this means that the space must be such that one can see the other whole, not only a part in close up. There must be enough space in which to interact, enough to 'play with' the possibilities, to create and develop that which is mutually satisfying. This concept of the *space between*, the area in which transactions take place, the space in which one's own view of oneself may undergo transition as it is mirrored in the other's face, the area for potentially creative interaction, we owe in different ways to Winnicott (1971) and Guntrip (1961). In this image, this metaphor, they bring to a consideration of couple relationships, 'parent-ness' and 'child-ness' in the process of growth and development within the world of other persons; openness and interplay, a trusting being together, as necessary to the human condition; the essence of personhood as being self-in-relation-to-other. No intimate, adult, heterosexual relationship, especially if maintained over the greater part of the couple's lifetime, can be perfect. It cannot be so for the individual, for the couple as a unit, for their families, for society at large, however much the imperfections may be denied. Winnicott's (1958) image of the best mother-child relationship as being 'good enough' seems an appropriate aim also for adults. These aspects of couple relationships, which we simplify within the frameworks of opportunities and obligations, choices and commitments, are expressions of mutuality and reciprocity. Such conditions are an essential feature of our model of marriage and they also, conceptually and in practice, influence our preferred model for marital work.

In the process of their development and maturation, in their achievement of the range of developmental tasks we have referred to, men and women as children and adolescents will have had experience of many crises, of many perceived threats to their sense of security, or identity or stability. They will have coped with these more or less, never wholly; and what from each of these phases remains unresolved, will be brought into marriage. A review of how the spouses have coped with some of the earlier crises in their lives can give some idea of how ready husband and wife were for marriage and how open they are to the possibilities of further maturation as persons in relationship. Such a view does not of itself resolve the choices which have to be made in creating change with a couple in their relationship, but it can be a contribution to an understanding and recognition of the complexity of some marital problems. An example from a particular couple might illustrate this: together with other quotations and examples used in our text, it is taken from the anonymized cases of couples with whom we have worked, either as practitioner or researcher.

John was a highly successful young businessman, well regarded by his peers according to him and his wife. His brusque efficiency did not wholly conceal his chronic anxiety and fear of failure. His wife Agnes, who had given up her nursing career on marriage, said her husband had never been interested in her. Amidst furious tears she said, 'He goes after everything, people and things. He never lets go. He'd fall apart if he had to give anything up. As for giving anything to anybody! And we have no sex life.' She had at first mothered him and been proud of him until some time after the sudden death of her father (the eldest of four daughters, she had been his favourite). As she searched for care and affection, John became even more self-absorbed and distant. Agnes' widowed mother persuaded them to move into her much larger family house. Gradually, she became openly critical of Agnes' attitude to John; it lacked respect, she said. And 'you wouldn't be like that if you remembered that one day you might be a widow too'. The crisis came for Agnes when John suggested that his elderly parents be assisted to purchase a small house nearby: 'You know Mum's depressed and it would be a great help to Dad if we let him do odd jobs for us around here. After all, I'm all they've got.' It was Agnes who had been referred for help by her general practitioner, but was the crisis particular to her; in what ways were husband and mother part of her problem; who or what might be said to have caused it? These are the kinds of issues which, in more general terms we shall explore.

COUPLE SYSTEMS AND CAUSES

In part 2, we looked at a range of ways in which men and women organize and institutionalize their long-term relationships. As we demonstrated, this unit, this particular system of interacting and relating parts, does not exist in isolation either in terms of time (because each couple represents a stage in the life history of their respective families) or in terms of current relationships (because each has other relationships in family, at work and at leisure). Nor however special it may seem to any couple (and specialness may be a positive or a negative experience) is it unique or wholly idiosyncratic. We have shown that there are different forms of this system and different ways of functioning. It is also part of everyday experience and knowledge that there are great differences in how husbands and wives relate to each other. Some marriages seem like parent-child pairs, others like brother and sister. Some appear to be between children or adolescents dressed up as adults and others between consenting grown-ups. Some appear to be held together by friendship and shared interests, others by constant conflict, differing in whether the focus of warfare is victory through attrition or the uncertainty of guerrilla attacks. In considering patterns of relationship, there is a greater readiness to describe behaviours and actions, rather than the ways in which spouses experience each other: emotions tend to be given more prominence than thoughts; issues of dominance-submission tend to be more familiar than those of independence-dependence, while the ways in which couples reach decisions or contend with each other's power are less readily addressed. Changes in patterns of full-time and part-time employment as they affect husbands and wives; changes in the ways in which income is received by the couple; questions of how couples use money and what this might convey about their relationship; these are topics rarely brought up in discussions about marital problems and even less often as issues to be focused on in attempts to resolve them. All of us carry a great deal of information about the ways in which couples relate, about the different kinds of couple system, some of it highly detailed. We may have opinions about the causes of these differences as we often have about the causes of problems in relationships. But whether we have evidence for these opinions or a sufficient understanding of possible causes is another matter.

Our understanding of why there are different patterns of couple relationships is as limited as our understanding of why particular kinds of couple develop particular problems in their relationship. We are on uncertain ground when we talk of one event, or experience, or behaviour being the cause of another. We do not greatly improve our understanding by talking of a constellation or series of events or behaviours. And we take a relatively small step forward by talking of predisposing and precipitating causes, of vulnerability and provocative factors. Questions of cause and effect influence our understanding not only of individuals, of couples, but of persons in wider networks or systems of relationships – families, groups, organizations, society at large. The answers we may arrive at in posing such questions will influence how and why we intervene in particular ways in seeking to help resolve the problems which couples may present. Is it correct that in our society, discussions about the causes of distress in personal relationships are less characterized than in the past by talk of blame and of fault? Even if it is, does that mean that we are less willing to allocate or define responsibility for what happens in a person's life or in relationships? The continuing debate within the field of family therapy about how to effect change in relationships, is to a significant degree determined by a shift from the concept of linear cause and effect mechanisms to one of circular causality, the idea that each person affects the other's behaviour in a continuing process, which may maintain the system, that is, the couple or family, in a stable state, or may induce change. These causes and the mechanisms for change are seen to lie in the system, part of its inherent nature, a concept that seems to challenge the view that the individual has any freedom to choose, or indeed any responsibility for the nature and consequences of choice. Arguments about cause and effect are neither new, nor peculiar to the world of relationships: they are a major theme within the discourses of philosophy and science. But practitioners asked and allowed to intervene in the lives of couples cannot wait until the resolution of these questions in their generality. They must take some form of action, even though concepts of cause and effect may have been inadequately examined and tested.

We recognize that our own view as presented here is limited, but we hope that in other sections of the book it will be extended and seen to fit experience. Our model of causation is historical and developmental, dynamic and contextual. It recognizes that there can be only rarely, if ever, 'one cause' for any marital problem, and further it emphasizes that the nature and process of causes is inevitably complex. We consider it idle, if no more, to pretend that the capacity to create and sustain relationships is not affected by temperament and constitution, by the capacities and limitations of our nature and genetic programming. It is a widely held view that children and young people who grow up with parents who are in constant and prolonged conflict, themselves have difficulty in establishing adequate relationships in adult life. There is much evidence to support this opinion (Rutter 1972; Hinde 1980). And we know also that the experience of loss and bereavement at particular stages of development may create the conditions which make marital conflict and difficulties more likely. While it can be said that not-fully-resolved emotional problems in early life may predispose to later relationship conflicts, there is very little evidence to link the different phases of development in adult life with particular kinds of marital problem. In addition, our model of causation is dynamic in expressing the view that no cause-effect can be once-for-all; no significant life experience exerts only a 'one-off' effect; no persons or relationships are in a state of total stasis, so that events and circumstances influence persons in a continuing process of change, however minimal. Our model of causation is also contextual in that our experience with couples shows how readily distress in relationships is closely linked, or associated, with what is experienced as happening in the external world. It is difficult to show or satisfactorily prove that the debates, arguments, conflicts about marriage and other couple relationships expressed within society are causes of marital problems. What is clear is that many couples are uncertain about what is to be regarded as normal or acceptable: in the way they share their lives and responsibilities, in their sexual relationship, in the ways they make decisions.

We recognize that what we have so far said about causes is likely to be debateable and subject to challenge. What is clear in our minds is the need for those who work with couples to have theories, concepts, ideas, about causes. Couples most certainly will have not so much ideas as *convictions* about cause, blame, fault, responsibility and what has to be done to put matters right. Causes are more likely to be equated by couples in difficulties with who is right and who is wrong, rather than with any issue of principle. In one way or another couples, if they are not to opt out of work with a therapist or counsellor at an early stage, need assuring that the programme of intervention proposed can lead to change for the better, and that what couple and therapist do together will be a cause of improvement.

Some therapists claim that more important than thinking about causes is exploring the meaning and the purpose of the particular problem presented, for example what is the meaning for a couple of his excessive alcohol consumption and her depressive mood; what purpose is derived in the maintenance of their relationship by the drinking-depressive mood; what would be the effect of the reduction of alcohol intake, or the relief from depression; and could one change cause the other, or make it worse? Such questions can shift energy and attention away from what can be stultifying attempts to define and understand causes, towards efforts to change the dynamics of the relationship. They may thus help to create change but they do not help to answer questions about causes or responsibility. We will return to these questions when considering ethical issues.

The search for causes, for an understanding of what leads to certain patterns of relationship or types of problem, is an expression of a need for order, for some kind of organization of our observations, to reduce complexity to apparently more manageable proportions. So too with our need to categorize and classify. While every couple relationship is in some senses unique and idiosyncratic, in others it has elements of what is societal, belonging to a particular social group or locality, and these characteristics refer also to the problems which may develop. As we implied in part 2, there are of course, both disadvantages and advantages in seeking to classify problems in marital relationships. Disadvantages include the risk of rigidity in thinking and in acting on the basis of classification. Stereotyping and crude labelling can conceal the individualities and identities of the couple so described. Well-grounded classifications summarize information, observation of opinion, help make sense of, give some meaning to the problems. They help differentiate one type or class of problem from another and act as a shorthand in conveying information to others. These include both professionals and couples who seek help and whose distress can be to some extent eased by knowing that they are not unique and that their type of form of problem can be understood, described, named. Unfortunately such a vocabulary and the terms which would be used in describing categories is still very limited. For medical (including psychiatric) problems there are extensive and increasingly refined systems of classification of illness or dysfunction, but this is far from the case with regard to marital relationships or problems. There is a great need for a system of classification which would first express and then transmit an understanding of the link between various forms of relationship and various presenting problems. Such a system would be multiaxial, taking account of forms of expression of relationship problems as well as possible causative factors and possible outcomes with or without intervention.

There are others, of course, who would disagree with such a

strategy. Some therapists and counsellors talk of the need to respect the uniqueness of each couple's problems, to be 'case specific'. They emphasize the need to focus on current issues, the 'here and now', the 'where they're at'. They point to the disadvantages of seeking for methods, techniques, skills which have a more general utility and appreciation. Our concern is that when carried to extremes this focus on specialness, this denial of categories and types, can lead to their being deprived of (or denying) what can be learned from finding the general in the particular, or failing to appreciate that lessons learned in working with particular couples can be applied in work with others – limitations which can seriously reduce what could be on offer to couples seeking help.

3.2 Issues in Intervention

Even as neighbour or friend, one would not respond to a couple distressed in their relationship without some idea, however vaguely articulated, of what might be called a good-enough marriage, or the kind of problems which can arise between persons in such a close relationship, or without some inkling of how one might try to be helpful. For the helper who purports to have either expertise or special commitment or both, more is required. Practitioners in marital work should be sufficiently well informed about the ways in which marriages may end and the possible reasons, particularly their sociological character. They need to be aware of what is permissible or possible by way of response and with what potential results. Their resources and skills should be such that they can respond effectively to a wide range of problems. It helps if all of that and more can be described, defined, identified by name; a name by which the activity, the experience, the relationship between couple and practitioner, may be known. As a title for this section, as well as a subtitle for the book, we chose the term *intervention*. We have used it in its sense of an activity between persons, between points of time, an activity which interposes. We see it as less specific than counselling or therapy, with less of a history attached to it. It is value free in the sense of not carrying meaning about the nature or purpose of the activity – though it suggests the idea of action or change. Where does one begin intervening in the life of couples who present problems: with a theory or conceptual framework, or more empirically, with the evidence, with the problems the couples bring? And given all the possibilities, what does one focus on? We have chosen in this section to focus on three main issues: models for marital work, ethical issues in practice and problems presented by couples. We do so because these are of interest and importance in themselves and also as an introduction to, a development towards, the way of working together with couples we call *consultation*.

MODELS FOR MARITAL WORK

Probably because marriage and other long-term adult relationships are so universal and at once so private and public, the attitudes, opinions and perspectives relating to them are accompanied by strong feelings and opinions. These readily give rise to stereotypes and ideologies about marriage and its problems and how these might be resolved; and this can be reflected in approaches to marital work. In considering different approaches we have used the term 'model', a term which describes a framework, an organization of concepts, a system of ideas or perceptions which seek to make sense of phenomena and experiences, as a basis for or guide to action. How best to present a range of models for marital work is beset with problems: there would probably be no ready agreement on how many discrete, recognizably different models should be considered. Each model which can be presented has variants which have developed as experience has been gained. Derived practice does not always seem to rest comfortably on the basis of concepts and any summary inevitably fails to do justice to what are complex systems of ideas and practice.

There are a number of publications in which different models are presented and to a greater or lesser degree, compared and contrasted. Paolino and McCrady (1978) explore both marriage and marital therapy from psychoanalytic, behavioural and systems-theory perspectives, though the authors who write about marriage are not those who write about the therapies derived from the theories. Their book also includes a review of research on the effectiveness of marital therapy and a critique and comparative analysis of the three approaches. Skynner (1980), within the much shorter compass of a journal article, compares psychodynamic, behavioural and systems models. He seeks particularly to integrate the psychoanalytic and systems perspectives and in discussing practice draws on the most widely accepted ideas from all the perspectives. To these, Dryden (1985) adds the rational-emotive and the behavioural-systems approaches, though the various approaches are not formally compared one with another. Even this list does not cover all the concepts or perspectives which determine practice. We have chosen briefly to explain the psychodynamic, behavioural, existential and systems models, in terms of some of their main features and of their similarities and differences. After reference to some of the issues in choosing a model for practice, that is, the need for development, we shall in the final section describe what we have called the consultative model (Haldane, McCluskey and Clark 1986).

The *psychodynamic model* derives from psychoanalysis, particularly object relations and group analytic theories. The work of Fairbairn (1952) is of central importance here, especially as developed by Dicks (1967), as is Bowlby's work on attachment and loss (Bowlby 1969, 1973, 1980). Other than Dicks' volume, the text which best presents the psychodynamic view of marital work is that by Skynner (1976). This perspective is concerned particularly with intrapsychic life, and the influence of the unconscious on action and on relationships. It explores the effect of personal and family histories on current experience and functioning and gives attention to the developmental life course of the couple, the events and experiences which have defined and shaped their relationship. A central notion is that marital problems express conflict, unconscious and unresolved, originating in the anxieties of childhood such as those which are associated with the attraction to one parent and the fear of the other's rivalry. While expressive of long-standing conflicts, being now experienced and acted out in the marital relationship, such problems also reveal evidence of the defence mechanisms which have been evolved to cope with associated feelings. These defence mechanisms, particularly those of denial, splitting and projection, are a necessary part of attempts to contain, if not resolve conflict. They create a status quo, a situation possibly more tolerable than that which is feared, so they are not readily altered. Couples to a greater or lesser degree take on the unresolved marital conflicts of their parents, and their children can be readily caught up in parents' defensive systems. The psychodynamic model is probably used more as a help towards understanding marital problems than as a basis for developing methods and techniques of intervention. Free association is not a method appropriate to the kind of conjoint therapy which is increasingly seen as most effective. The interpretation of the transference phenomena and experiences as they affect therapist and each individual, are of less immediate import than the exploration and interpretation of the relationship between husband and wife. This is not at all to infer that such experiences between therapist and one spouse may not, when understood, highlight and clarify, even explain aspects of the relationship between husband and wife. A constant search for clarification, even when this means confronting the couple with observations which may be experienced as distressing and the necessarily long process of working through defensive systems and conflicts, are however as relevant in couple work as with individuals.

While the origins of the psychodynamic model are essentially biological, those of the *behavioural model* are based in empirical science. Walker summarizes the behavioural approach to treatment as characterized by:

(1) commitment to objective methods;
(2) analysis and treatment of the target behaviour in relation to the environment in which it occurs;
(3) dependence on, and feed back into, experimental psychology and experimental psychopathology;
(4) precise and detailed objective specification of the target problem(s) and aims of 'treatment';
(5) precise and detailed specification of the techniques to be used;
(6) commitment to empirical monitoring and evaluation of each intervention in terms of (4) above. (Walker 1982:38)

Crowe (1985) from a rigorous research-cum-practice base, has illustrated the ways in which the behavioural model has developed and the indications for different types of intervention, in a volume (Dryden 1985) in which there is also a chapter on the behavioural approach and a commentary on other approaches (Mackay 1985). Quite apart from the increasing sophistication and range of application of the ideas and techniques particular to the various forms of behavioural therapy, the model has greatly influenced other forms of practice. The acceptance of the couple's stated problems as the focus for attention; the value of negotiating an agreement with the couple on the aims and methods of the work to be done; constant clarification of aims and objectives; monitoring of progress; and an emphasis on the improvement of communication: these are not peculiar to behavioural marital therapy, but their incorporation into other forms of practice owes much to the model.

The *existential model* owes more to philosophy than to science. We have written about existentialism as a model for psychotherapy (Haldane 1982), in relation to family therapy (Haldane and McCluskey 1982) and as a perspective in developing a consultative model for marital work (Haldane, McCluskey and Clark 1986). Existentialism has been concerned with experiences of living, such as loneliness, alienation, meaninglessness and despair, the fear of living fully and freely, the certainty of dying. It emphasizes the human search for meaning, the person's constant interactions with others in seeking to realize full potential, the need to take responsibility for shaping one's future. Those developments in existential philosophy which led to the emergence of the humanistic psychology movement have emphasized the individual's capacity for energy and growth, along with the need for and right to spontaneity and the joy of being creatively alive in the present. Existential therapies are concerned primarily with the inner world of persons, with internal experiences of self and of self in relation to others. Thus in method they are introspective and reflective, involving a continuing scrutiny of thoughts, feeling states, experiences, imaginings and associated somatic experiences. This focus on self might seem unlikely to be helpful in work with couples, yet the work of Rogers (1961), which belongs to the world of existential ideas, has greatly influenced the practice of counselling in the marriage guidance movement. Our own experience of work with couples shows that this kind of exploration of self undertaken in the presence of the spouse and within the context of problems in the marital relationship, can create the conditions necessary for change and enrich that process.

The *systems model*, which has so greatly influenced work with families and couples, is a relatively recent development (hardly more than a generation) in therapy and counselling. Though the basic ideas were not then new, a general systems theory was first proposed by Von Bertalanffy (1973) in the 1940s. This is a theory of the interrelatedness and interdependence of parts and wholes in their structure, functioning, relationships and capacity for change. Its emphasis is on circular rather than linear causality, with the consequence that the functioning of the system can be changed by intervention at any one of a number of transactions within it. This perspective recognizes that structure is evident in related series of events and patterns of activity, over a period of time in the life of individuals in relationship. Less concerned than the psychodynamic model with the inner world of persons, the systems model focuses particularly on the transactions across the boundaries which identify, define and differentiate the parts of the system – individual, couple, family, wider social network. Such transactions are important in the regulation of the system and to its capacity for adaptation and change as a continuing process. As with other conceptual frameworks, systems theory as applied to family and marital work has developed a number of 'schools' or approaches, well summarized by Barker (1987). In general, intervention is actively problem solving and change inducing. The practition-er may function as the interpreter, facilitator, of the psychodynamic model, or be even more of an entrepreneurial conductor and director than the behavioural therapist. Most of the literature which applies theories of systems to marital work is based on therapy with couples. But an important contribution to understanding the organization of marital work in the context of services and agencies comes from the staff of the Tavistock Institute of Human Relations who have been concerned with the study of groups, institutions and organizations (Bion 1961; Miller 1976; Bridger, 1981).

That there are similarities and differences between these models will be evident from this brief sketch, but some of the variations need further elaboration. In general the psychodynamic and existential models require of practitioner and couple a more reflective, explora-tory mode than the others. In those others, the practitioner is more likely to be directive, more likely to plan or actively define with the couple an agenda and programme for their joint activity. The psychodynamic, existential and some forms of the systems model attend to the inner world of persons, to intrapsychic areas of functioning, to the unconscious, to feeling states; the majority of the behavioural approaches not at all. Behavioural and systems models have been particularly concerned to define methods and techniques and especially in the former, regularly to monitor the results of their application. All are concerned to assist the couple to change, but whereas the psychodynamic and existential tend to see change as a consequence of developing understanding and insight, the others are concerned as early as possible and by a range of methods, to induce change in the couple's behaviour, their ways of relating, their rules of engagement. Practitioners of the systems and behavioural models have been particularly productive in defining the skills required and in evaluating their applications by means of supervisory methods, such as observation through one-way screens or by television moni-toring. Distinctions about the focus of the work being the present, the 'here and now' of what is observed of the couple together, compared with exploration and reflection of the influence of past experience on present relationships, can be more apparent in principle than in practice. But it can be said that the behavioural model focuses unequivocally on present behaviour and how it can be changed; some systems approaches also do so, while others are more like the psychodynamic model in seeking to understand the influence of past on present and helping couples free themselves of particular patterns of relating, behaving, communicating.

There does seem to be emerging a consensus of opinion which might form the basis for a definition of best practice. Most would agree that so far as possible, the nature, duration and aim of the work to be done together should be explored and negotiated with husband and wife. This is an always complex, frequently difficult and some-times prolonged process. Even when agreement, contract and com-mitment are achieved they may need to be reviewed and renegoti-ated, depending on progress. There is a move towards being more specific, less global, more realistic about aims; to being less open-ended or vague about expectations. Ways of helping husband and wife to understand each other, to express themselves more effectively to each other, to resolve problems jointly, to be able to recognize and mutually reward each other's qualities and contributions, these are central to each of the models, though the methods and processes of achieving them are very different. There is increasing agreement that husband and wife be seen together and that if for some reason this is not done, the focus should be on the relationship rather than on the problems or conflicts particular to each of the spouses. Systems and behavioural practitioners tend to plan for a specific number of sessions and to have a relatively short-term programme of interven-tion (though the definition of 'short-term' will vary). While some would insist that most work with couples needs to be long-term, most would agree that from the beginning, husband, wife and practitioner know that the work together must end and have an idea about how to agree on its timing.

MAKING CHOICES

These models represent different perspectives on personal rela-tionships, different ways of construing meaning, different approaches to change and how best to achieve it. The claims for these different models have prompted difference and competiton, argu-ments about which is best, but too rarely, research which seeks to compare the effectiveness of particular practices in helping to resolve particular kinds of marital problems. Fortunately research en-deavours seem to be moving in this direction. There seems to be a greater recognition that no one model is appropriate for all purposes and that all have something to contribute to the understanding and resolution of marital problems. Practitioners' descriptions of their work seem rarely derived from one particular theoretical position or conceptual framework, nor primarily from empirical data or from formal research, but much more from accumulated experience. Most seem to be pragmatic in their practice, as much concerned with the integrity of their work and their relationships with couples as they are with the need to have any over-arching theory or universally applicable model. But even this recognition does not deprive the practitioner of the responsibility of making some choice. Personal inclination and personal history, ways of construing the world, basic training and professional experience will be deciding factors as much as, probably more than, any formal evaluation of the work, any systematic examination of the application of theory to practice. And while ethical judgements may not often be, or appear to be, significant factors in the choices made, we find it unrealistic to think that such choices are in any sense value free.

All of these models have contributed to the development of activities called marital therapy or counselling. It is not always clear whether there are differences between these two activities and if so what they are. Practitioners are called therapists or counsellors; husbands and wives become patients or clients and much energy has been spent on explaining how these terms should be used or what are their limitations. In this already complex situation, it may appear unwise and unrealistic to propose yet another model, but we think the attempt is justified. What we shall propose is neither original, nor a radical departure from current thinking and practice, but a development which sees the face-to-face encounters of practice within the contexts of the public aspects of marriage and the organization of services.

DEVELOPING A DIFFERENT MODEL

Any framework for practice in marital work should be concerned less with individuals, their development and their life stage and more with persons-in-relationship, with couples, in the wider context of their family and social life. It should recognize how much of adult life is concerned with evolving and changing pair relationships, with the making and breaking of affectional bonds (Bowlby 1979), with the constitution, dissolution, resolution, of important, interdependent relationships, whatever their degree of intimacy. It should be relevant to a range of problems which can occur in couple relationships at their various stages. These include the transition from courtship or cohabitation to the early years of marriage, particularly the phase which follows the birth of the first child. They include the recurring possibility of dissolution or breakdown in the relationship and not only those in some way signalled as a prelude to separation or divorce. As we saw in part 2, few couples experience with equanimity the process of separation or divorce and its aftermath and many talk of how the trauma of these experiences interferes with attempts to form new relationships. Despite public awareness of the consequences of divorce, for most people remarriage (possibly also reconstituting a family) remains a highly personalized private trouble, to be handled alone. The problems of marriage in later life, for those who are retired (that is, for an increasing proportion of the population), have been inadequately addressed: deteriorating physical or mental health in one spouse makes great demands on a relationship and for those whose marriage has not ended in divorce, the inevitable ending for others is the loss of the spouse by death. All these problems have to a greater or lesser degree, elements of the experiences described in the titles of Bowlby's three volumes elaborating his attachment theory and its consequences: *Attachment and Loss* (1969); *Separation; anxiety and anger* (1973); *Loss; sadness and depression* (1980).

The majority of spouses or couples who seek help in resolving problems in their relationships are not by any definition ill and should not be called patients, that is, defined into a role which too often creates a degree and type of dependency which is not consistent with accepting responsibility for change in oneself and one's relationships. This is not to say that one, even both spouses, may not need treatment for an illness as well as, or instead of, help with the problem they present. But it is important that models for marital work are not constrained by concepts of pathology and illness.

To be capable of any reasonably comprehensive application in practice, a model should not be restrictive in its focus. It should not be constrictive in the modes of working together used by couple and practitioner. There should be time and space and opportunity for listening and for talking, but also for role-playing, homework assignments, drawing or painting or modelling, that is, for a range of activities which enlarge the capacity of the participants to express themselves and to communicate with each other.

Those who seek help for their marital problems are adults and there is a range of freedoms and responsibilities to be recognized. So a generally acceptable model should be characterized by a concern for negotiation, a continuing process of exploration, review and evaluation about the issues on which the couples wish to work, the experiences or behaviours which they seek to change. While focusing on the couple and their life together it should be possible also to take account of and respond to the ways in which couples manage 'external' factors which impinge upon their relationship, such as their experience of families or the images of marriage current in society. One test of a model for practice should also be that it should help towards reducing the number of currently separate services, or modes of working. The effects of this separation range from duplication of effort to competition for resources, from generalist approaches to specialisms which further enhance the tendency to separate. We shall take up these issues again in parts 4 and 5 but here we emphasize the search for a model which would reduce the need for apparently mutually exclusive terms such as premarital counselling, marital therapy, marriage guidance, marriage counselling, divorce counselling, conciliation, and which could be applied in practice in the various settings and life stages described by these terms. Not least, the development of any model for marital work should take account of and make use of those ideas, methods and techniques shared by the perspectives and practices already described. Our interest is in developing a *consultative* model.

ETHICAL ISSUES IN PRACTICE

We use the term 'ethical issues' in reference to aspects of practice which give rise to questions such as right and wrong behaviour, values and standards, obligations and responsibilities, means and ends, openness and concealment; and which affects each of the individuals and the various relationships which exist within the practitioner-couple triad. In recent years, practitioners in the 'caring professions' in general and those in particular who practise some form of psychological treatment, have become more concerned with ethical aspects of their work. This is at least to some extent due to comments and criticisms from clients and patients, as individuals or in their membership of various kinds of pressure group. At the same time, moral philosophers have become more willing to attend to such dilemmas, to apply ethical principles to the everday choices which have to be made in practice. But there is so far little evidence of the kind of collaboration between philosophers and practitioners which could develop ethical guidelines for marital counselling and therapy. While there has been a steadily expanding literature on ethical aspects of the psychotherapies, counselling, casework and more recently on family therapy, there is much less on marital work. The reasons for this lack are not clear. Perhaps it is assumed that the ethical aspects of practice with individuals can simply be transferred to that with couples, just as texts on family therapy often regard marital work as but an aspect or subsystem of family work. Perhaps it is because, as we shall see (in the United Kingdom at least), those whose stated priority is work with couples (i.e. marriage guidance counsellors) are still for the most part, voluntary, unpaid, part-timers, functioning in relative privacy, relatively rarely as members of a multidisciplinary organization. On the other hand, those professionals whose work is more open to public scrutiny (doctors, social workers, psychologists) in a very few settings indicate even an interest in marital work, far less give it priority. So that in whatever kind of setting it is practised, marital counselling or therapy does not readily command the kind of public awareness or interest which might lead to debate about the ethical aspects of practice. Perhaps it is because the subject of marriage is seen as in complex ways so affected, even constrained by ethical considerations, that these are not regarded as the proper concern of practitioners, who thus, in seeking to help resolve marital problems, simplify them by ignoring or denying their ethical aspects.

As we saw in part 2, there is in our society continuing and increasingly open debate about what is 'normal', 'healthy' and 'acceptable' in the marital relationship. Arguments between husband and wife about what is the normal frequency of sexual intercourse; disagreement about whether the aggressive expression of opinion is healthy; differences about the acceptability of spouses' extramarital relationships: these reflect the range of opinion (and practice) and for couple and practitioner they pose questions about the assumptions and values which are brought to their encounter. Opinions about divorce and remarriage are strongly held, but there is no evidence to indicate to what degree the range of opinion at any one time current in society is reflected in the membership of any group of personnel undertaking marital work; our experience however is that what may be publicly expressed as policy does not always match up to practitioners' responses to individuals in the process of such change in their marital relationships. Similarly, debates about gender equality and the way these influence couple relationships, employment practices, financial affairs, legally defined standards, have aspects which are political, social, psychological, but also ethical, and will colour the content and process of marital work. As a society we remain ambivalent about whether marriage is to be regarded as a matter of private responsibility or public concern.

In such a context practitioners will have personal, if not uniquely idiosyncratic views on the nature, purpose and values of the marital state and the experiences and behaviours which within it should be regarded as normal or acceptable. Such personal standards, linked with the particular theoretical framework and training which are brought to the work, always carry the risk that what is offered and the aims set, are too determined by personal ideology. 'I may have feelings about the matter, but in my role as counsellor, whether or not a couple stay married or separate is an issue on which I must remain neutral,' is not, as it is often thought to be, a detached and value-free stance; it is one which risks splitting off the exercise of skills and methods from the personal attributes of counsellor or therapist. Such a process deprives the couple of a resource known to make significant contribution to the achievement of beneficial change. 'Couples must be free to make their own decisions and only they can take responsibility for their actions,' may at first seem ethically defensible and good practice, but is at best a limited statement and does not absolve the practitioner from his or her responsibility in influencing process and outcome in particular ways. In our view, those who work with couples have a responsibility and an obligation to develop a framework within which to examine ethical aspects of practice and to keep these under review. Such topics can be included in the consultation and supervision which belong to continuing training; and their consideration would be improved if from time to time moral philosophers were to contribute.

Central to this kind of intervention, of which marital work is one class, is respect for persons, in their uniqueness, their differentiation from others, their integrity. This can be stated as a basic principle, representing as it does a particular ethical perspective. Work with individuals is not always as easy to practise as to define; in marital work it is still more complicated: how to be even-handed, give equal attention to each spouse, not favour the case of one against the other, especially how not to promote the interests of one against the other. Each spouse has a problem, a need, a priority, even a demand, to present in the presence of the other, or at least regarding the relationship with the other: 'I want you to help my husband realize he can't do as he wants. Will you do that for me?' is a loaded question and request. Husband or wife seek an alliance of some kind with counsellor or therapist, with a stranger already clothed in expectation before the first meeting. How to be fair to each, especially when one's own feelings are engaged or when one may approve of, or support, or agree with, one spouse more than the other? As couples work towards a resolution of their problems, conflicts are expressed and identified, others may be revealed for the first time, and yet others might be created as one spouse changes in ways different from the other and not at the same pace – especially when such differences have not been anticipated. Wife to husband: 'If you really want my opinion, I don't think this is doing us any good. You're not so sex-mad as you were, but you don't look after me any more.' Husband to therapist in response: 'Can't she see I don't want any more to be her baby-daddy. I need to see you on my own to get out of this.' These are complicated messages, requiring the practitioner to make choices, take decisions which have technical components in the 'how' to respond, and ethical considerations in the 'why' and 'with what aim'. Some couples seeking help agree that both want the marriage to continue, but this aim may not survive. It can become evident that each spouse has a different agenda for a future in the marriage, that each wants to continue to work with counsellor or therapist. How does the practitioner take adequate account of the rights and needs of one in relation to those of the other, while maintaining his or her own responsibilities and competence? The issue of confidentiality in a particular form, may appear to pose problems for the practitioner. Sometimes a spouse seen alone, will ask the counsellor not to share particular information with the other: 'I think that's best forgotten' or 'It won't really help for her to know,' are invitations to a collusive secrecy, a coalition of power in which something is denied to the other spouse, a game into which some may be easily seduced. Agreement to such a ploy both limits what the practitioner may be able to do and puts in question any principles of openness.

Respect for individuality needs to be accompanied by a respect for the nature and dynamic of each couple relationship. Experience shows how often that which is complained of, for example, neglect, violence, isolation, is also that which seems most difficult to change, which is the status quo, and therefore satisfying in some particulars to both husband and wife. What seems for any couple to be acceptable, even satisfying, may be in important respects very different from the practitioner's view of what is normal and acceptable or – to an even greater degree – what the practitioner considers desirable and ideal. Such potential discrepancies which, if not resolved, can interfere with adequate resolution, require practitioner and couple to reach sufficient understanding about what is hoped for and attainable. Such an understanding might in principle seem a necessary prerequisite to treatment: in practice it might represent a successful achievement and ending. In a similar way, the practitioner's responsibility to explain what he or she is doing and aims to achieve, is a necessary expression of openness and invitation to collaboration, but the process may not be completed until closure is agreed. One particular type of closure is a recurring theme in all marital work: what are the conditions or principles which determine that the aim of marital work should be a continuation of the marriage and what conditions legitimize the aim, or consequence, of separation and divorce? As we shall explore further in part 4, the early years of the marriage guidance movement emphasized the aim of helping couples stay together, of saving marriages. As views about marriage and divorce have changed, this emphasis has been modified: separation and divorce have come to be regarded as acceptable outcomes, just as those who are unmarried or have been divorced can now become marriage guidance counsellors. There is always the possibility that this more open, accepting view conceals a degree of ambivalence in the practitioner, which matches that in the couple, a state which may severely limit the effective use of carefully developed skills.

So far we have briefly explored some of the ethical issues as they affect couple and practitioner. But each part of this system has an external world, the interaction with which may express or raise further ethical problems. Should a couple be expected to stay together for the sake of the children; do members of the extended families have any rights, or contributions to make in the resolution of the couple's problems, and what responsibility does the practitioner have in these matters? To whom counsellors and therapists are accountable, and for what aspects of their work, is determined primarily by organizational and managerial policies, together with definitions of what may be regarded as professional autonomy. There is no organization in the United Kingdom which has tried to define ethical principles or guidelines for marital therapy or counselling, an interesting lack when we consider that the greater part of such work takes place within marriage guidance councils which are approved, sanctioned and, to a large extent, funded by the state. What responsibility do practitioners have to take account of public expectations, even if these can with confidence be identified, and what right does society have to expect them to have aims consistent with 'current norms'? These are not questions to which practitioners have so far been required to find answers, but as public funding becomes increasingly conditional, such demands may be made.

There are important issues here about power and authority. The influence which the practitioner can have on the life of a couple, derives partly from the authority implicitly or explicitly given by the couple and by the employing agency or service, and comes partly from the individual's competence and sense of confidence in the work. The practitioner has the power to define the rules of the encounter, to control the nature and flow of information within it, to maintain its confidentiality. Some of this power may be regarded as necessary to the proper control of the process, but the consequences of such a view may be more restricting than enabling.

PROBLEMS PRESENTED BY COUPLES

In part 2 we looked at some of the ways in which marital problems are constructed and explored, how these are influenced by history and changing ideologies. In part 4 we shall discuss the difficulties which wives, husbands and couples encounter in the process of seeking help, the procedures and organizational impediments which they may have to overcome before meeting the person who will actively engage with them in the process of change. Such difficulties, as we shall show, are not to be taken lightly and may add to those already being experienced in the relationship. Here, we shall restrict our attention to the problems presented by the couple.

We use the term 'problem' in its dictionary meaning of bone of contention, subject of dispute, puzzle, mystery, dilemma, predica- ment, quandary. The phrase 'presenting problem' belongs to the language of the medical profession, which one of us has been accustomed to using. It conveys that a person brings something, offers it for attention and scrutiny; and also the sense that what is brought is a first statement, an introduction to something possibly deeper and more complex. 'Problem' is also a term which wives and husbands often use when they first seek help. Other terms such as breakdown, dysfunction, disorder, disharmony, symptoms, are no more precise and carry connotations about conceptual frameworks which can be limiting rather than illuminating.

Wives, more often than husbands, initiate the search for help and when only one spouse attends, it is usually the wife. Studies such as those of Brannen and Collard (1982) and of Hunt (1985) have shown that, in general, wives and husbands do not share the same aim in their search, wives tending to look for emotional support and husbands for advice about action. Such hopes and expectations reflect what are currently criticized as gender stereotypes. It is difficult to know to what extent these research findings have affected the perception of practitioners in their assessment, far less the question of what kind of responses should be available. As we indicated in part 2, it is important to keep in mind that 'marital problems' may be experienced very differently by men and women.

Both practitioners and researchers remain relatively ignorant about the incidence and prevalence of the various expressions of marital problems and even more so about any kind of rank order of the frequency of particular presentations. The order in which we discuss how problems are presented does not imply any such hierarchy: instead we begin with what is personal to the individual, then consider couple and family and finally refer briefly to how private dilemmas may be expressed through the language of public debate.

A somatic symptom, or complaint, may be the first signal that all is not well in a relationship. It may be about a discomfort, an ache, a pain, anywhere in the body and sometimes in several places at once. The complaint may seem evidently associated with the relationship, for example some specific unease or discomfort which accompanies sexual activity, but less specific pains are not uncommon and may be disabling. Spouses may bring an anxiety or complaint about the other: about neglect or violence or unfaithfulness, all of which may take a variety of forms; about too much alcohol; about neglect of the children. Or they may express disagreement and conflict: about their sexual life, or parenting, or time spent with other people, or money. Some feel trapped and seek advice on whether to stay or leave, or whichever is decided, how to hold to it. Concern for the other can be very close to the feeling that it is 'really' him or her who is to blame. Just as one spouse may present the other as *the* problem so they, or more usually the wife, may bring for attention the emotional state, relationships, health, of a child or adolescent. 'If only she weren't always ill / he didn't spend so much time away from home' is a complaint or plea for change complex enough. It becomes more so when the anxiety or anger is complained of in 'if only he didn't mix with these hooligans / she would let me know when she's going to be away all night, we'd be a happy couple and not argue like we do now.' Nor is the complexity reduced by the plea and generous offer which says 'It's our daughter who really needs to see you and you can be sure we'll do all we can to help.' Some marriages seem to become the battleground for the acting out of current public agendas, in which instead of playing the roles scripted for them by their personal and family histories, spouses behave like the stereotypes portrayed in so many media debates: 'I don't see why she should go back to work after she's had the baby' or 'We each have a right to be independent in our financial affairs' or 'I don't see why we should assume I'm the one to get sterilized; I'm the one who had to use the pill.' Some of these conflicts are, of course, not new, but the ways in which they are expressed mean that it may take some time to work through the rhetoric and begin working with the persons whose lives are intimately interlocked.

It may be difficult to show that the cause of severe and chronic pain may be emotional conflict and tension rather than a disorder of joint or muscle; to persuade parents that there are problems in their relationship of which their offspring's condition is a sign; that both need to be involved if a relationship problem is to be resolved; and none of these views can be justified without adequate assessment. So it may take several steps for a couple to acknowledge that the primary problem is in their experience of each other, or the way they behave towards each other, or the lack of understanding between them. Even when a couple attend together, agreed that they have a problem in their marriage, that they seek help to change and want each to contribute to improvement, the practitioner must keep in mind that while the problem may express and define conflict, its purpose is not always evident. Expressed problems may be signals of distress: they may also represent a defensive state, a means of concealing or avoiding, or preventing some state perceived, however, dimly, as potentially worse. A pain in the neck may be more tolerable than one's unacceptable, feared, anger; excess drinking may seem safer than the underlying depression; distressing quarrels over the children's behaviour may be the only way of maintaining liveliness in a relationship otherwise dead. So the presenting problem, however important it is and however much it may remain the focus of attention, is usually but a beginning.

3.3 Consultation

Like 'therapy' and 'counselling', the term 'consultation' is well known and in regular use, but with various meanings. A common usage is with regard to the doctor-patient relationship. Patients seek a consultation with a doctor, usually their general practitioner. In the National Health Service 'consultant' describes a hospital-based medical practitioner senior in the staff hierarchy, a statement and description of status and responsibility as much as a description of function.

The model of consultation we wish to elaborate is derived from the work of Harold Bridger. He describes a main dimension of his work in recent years as: 'developing strategies for organisational review and design which entail joint collaboration in working through issues of changing tasks and changing environmental conditions. A special feature of such collaborative working with the complex inter-relationship of people, structures, technologies and tasks, is that the organisation builds its own capacity to deal more effectively with containing change, future imbalance and uncertainty' (Bridger 1981:np).

Bridger suggests a number of models for consultation. In the 'Engineering Model' the consultant uses knowledge and skills in a particular field of work to help clarify and define a problem and develop a plan to improve the situation. 'The problem is, in effect, "taken away" from the client and is handed back in a better (or "bandaged") state – and usually with a report including recom-mendations or solutions' (ibid.:26). The 'Teaching Model' is a variant of this: 'the consultant collects the data, thinks through some options and alternative solutions and, through his explanations and argu-ments, convinces the client of what he should do' (ibid.:27). A more apparently collaborative model aims to achieve change for the client's own good. This collaborative form 'is a front for dealing with expected or actual resistance to what the consultant may wish to propose. Various coercive or manipulative devices may be employed to achieve what the consultant wants the client to do' (ibid.:27). This is essentially a 'Consultant-centred Model'. The shift towards a 'Client-centred Model' involves the 'client' (be that individual, cou-ple, group, organization) as well as the consultant, being kept in touch with and able to take on the responsibility for developing insights, coping with conflicts and turbulent feelings, creating new solutions to client problems. 'Increasingly, whether in psychother-apeutic, social or organisational contexts, this degree of client involve-ment implies a corresponding attention to the situation and process within which the consulting or counselling takes place. Appropriate facilitating transitional conditions will, therefore, need to be created to ensure the optional utilisation of the client's inner resources and potential' (ibid.:27). This approach involves a significant shift in the consultant's role – using his or her skills and resources to identify and promote those of the client (or client system) in working through the problem, formulating and acting on decisions and building in re-sources for continuing to live with the consequences of these deci-sions. An aspect or development of this approach is a 'Collaborative Model', 'which involves a greater share of tasks in some critical endeavour or longer term planning' (ibid.:27). In this way of working with persons in some form of personal or organizational relationship, the consultant must listen and learn with the client.

It will be evident that each of these ways of working with clients could find application in marital work. In the practice of the collaborative model, there is no doubt often an element of giving advice or teaching and always there is a danger that the consultant's collaboration is more pseudo than genuine. Bridger's ideas and descriptions of practice appeal to us for a number of reasons. They bring together in an integrated way theory and practice from psychoanalysis, particularly object-relations theory, and socio-technical systems. They resonate with much of existential philosophy and its concern with the developing self in the context of personal relations. Learning as essential to the process of change, is a central feature. It is not constrained by concepts of dysfunction or deviance, illness or pathology, or with that which is limiting. Rather a central assumption is that in a genuinely collaborative setting, potential can be realized, learning take place and positive change become established. Particularly important is the implication that these ideas can be applied in a consistent way in therapeutic settings, in research and in consultation to organizations. In this last section of part 3, our focus will be on face-to-face encounters with couples, with husbands and wives who seek help in the resolution of problems in their marriage. We shall explore these in the context of this model of consultation. In parts 4 and 5 we shall look further at applications to research and to organizational development.

THE FIRST CONSULTATION

In an earlier section we discussed some of the ways in which marital problems might be presented and showed that a proportion of these will in the first instance present in some other guise indirectly, for example, as a physical symptom or as a concern or a complaint about another person. Clearly we cannot describe a pattern for initial contact which would be appropriate for all those variations. What we are concerned with in this section is the first meeting between spouse or couple and the person who is accepted as having defined the problem as marital or has indicated willingness to help. That might be the person of first contact, such as the general practitioner, social worker or marriage guidance counsellor. It might also be someone to whom a general practitioner has referred spouse or couple. We are therefore talking of the situation in which a marital problem has been identified and acknowledged, however tentatively.

We do not call this first meeting an interview, because that term has the connotation that the main purpose is for information to be given, usually in one direction, from interviewee to interviewer. Nor do we consider it appropriate to talk of an intake interview, in which a staff member or team has a function of allocating the couple to some other member or group to take on therapy, or counselling, or casework. We consider that in general those who undertake such first consultations, should be in a position to take responsibility for whatever is offered at their conclusion, that is, they should be expected to be capable of negotiating beginning, middle and end stages in relationships; of constitution, resolution and dissolution of relationships. We say 'in general', because we recognize that no one consultant, or one organization, may be able to offer the range of responses required by the couples who come their way. We explore these issues further when looking at the aims of the first consultation.

If this work is to be done adequately, attention must be given to organizing an appropriate *setting*. There must be enough space for the three persons to sit comfortably and also to move around the room if necessary. Undue clutter, a room with an excessive air of busyness, can be a distraction. Quietness is needed, both from general background noise and from interruptions, either at the door or from the telephone. The consultant has particular responsibility for ensuring lack of interruption and for being able to tell the couple that the time they have together will not be interrupted. In these senses the consultant creates a quiet territory in which full attention can be given to the couple and their problems and takes responsibility for maintaining the boundaries which define and enclose it. Time must be offered for the session, sufficient time for the couple to become accustomed to the setting, for the problems to be expressed, defined and explored and for decisions to be reached. The couple should not have to think 'How much time do we have to say everything we want to say?' The consultant should arrive on time for the appointment and at an early stage in the 'settling down' process indicate clearly the time available, during which work on the couple's problems has absolute priority. To define the time boundary in this way, defines also a beginning and an ending, anticipates that whatever happens during the session there is an exit, an anticipated time for leaving, and gives further structure and form to the encounter. The duration of the time available will vary: most practitioners will consider an hour sufficient, some prefer one-and-a-half hours for the first meeting. The setting established should be such as to contribute to the couple's sense of feeling safe, of being given sufficient time and attention, of being held and protected at a time of considerable stress. These patterns should characterize all subsequent sessions, but they are particularly important for the first. At that meeting most couples are in crisis, often feeling desperate, hoping for the best while expecting the worst, their resources limited. It may be the first time for a long period that they have talked to each other, far less listened to each other and the first time that someone has concentrated attention on them. This is at once a hopeful and a daunting experience, because so many couples invest in it such high expectations, especially those who see it as a 'last chance'.

The primary *aim* of the first consultation is to terminate it with couple and consultant sufficiently agreed on the nature and purpose of the further action to be taken and by whom, based on a sufficient mutual understanding of the problems presented. We use the term 'sufficient' in recognition of the reality that both agreement and understanding may be partial and provisional. We do not think that a primary aim is to make this the first of several sessions, the laying of the basis for longer term work (who knows at the beginning that this would be appropriate or acceptable?) Nor do we consider that a primary aim is to present or encourage couples to express their most private thoughts and feelings (they may never have done this to each other, or perhaps only in their quarrels) so it should not be assumed that they can or ought to be able to do so in their first meeting with a stranger. Within this general aim the consultant must set himself or herself a number of objectives. There must be sufficient time for the couple to say what they want to say in *their* way. Any further information necessary to an understanding of the problems must be obtained in ways in which the couple feel they are contributing to the process. Husband and wife need to be told what can or cannot be offered in response to reasons given. Negotiation and exploration are required to find out what consultant and any particular husband and wife can do together, and the consultant must accept responsibility for seeking agreement on the next stage of action.

This first meeting is concerned primarily with *assessment* of the problem. The term diagnosis, properly used, would suffice, but it has come to be associated almost wholly with medical work, often negatively and sometimes inappropriately given a meaning which conveys a restricted way of thinking. Assessment is a process both incomplete and limiting if it is no more than identifying and naming a condition or state (helpful though that can be) and prescribing action. It should include couple and consultant seeking to make sense of the problems presented, to find some meaning in them, to identify the possibilities for resolution. It is not helpful only to seek simplification of the problem and where it is possible to identify and differentiate aspects of the problem this should be within the context that all marital problems are complex.

There is debate about whether such aims require one to 'take a history', to seek information about the couple's past life, or whether it is enough to focus on the present, on the 'here and now'; and debate continues about whether information is best obtained and systematized by history taking, by questionnaire, or by check list. This is, or should be, a debate about emphasis and not about limited or exclusive ways of arriving at some assessment of the problem. It may indeed be that in the first session the essence of the problem becomes evident from observations of how the couple behave and relate to each other. And it can be that an unduly assiduous search for information about the past diverts attention from what is evident and requiring recognition. Our view is that an assessment is incomplete unless attention is paid both to history and to present state. If a history is to be sufficient it will include: (1) information about the ways in which and over what period the presenting problem has developed; (2) the duration, quality, features of the relationship, how it began, the ways in which it has changed; (3) the history of the individuals before the couple relationship began, particularly of earlier intimate relationships; (4) information about the marriages of parents and others in the extended families. It is not only the facts of these histories which are important: it is also the couple's views of the facts, their experience of them and how they react now at a time of crisis to such recollections. Apart from listening to what the couple spontaneously wish to say about their past and asking systematic questions, which in a general way will develop a history over time, there are ways of focusing on highlights of the history, for example: (1) seeking information on what the couple regard as crises in their individual lives and relationship; (2) focusing on what they regard as important times or experiences in their own development; (3) drawing out a geneogram, or family tree, using this as a stimulus to recollection, a way of exploring the past and a method of comparing and contrasting the couples' relationship with others in their families.

Some general points can be made about assessment of the present relationship. It is essential to listen, pay attention to what is said, to the content and tone, to the words and the language and the feelings conveyed, that is, to have the couple expressing their individual thoughts and feelings, their attitudes to and experience of each other. It is important also to observe other ways in which they express and communicate, by gesture, posture, bodily movement, recognizing that these modes are often much more eloquent and accurate representations of inner life than words, and often ignored or denied in one spouse's recognition of the other. Such observations of the somatic state, of body language, are useful in acquiring information on the couple and also potentially, as a focus for attention in later sessions: working on modification of bodily communication may be a more effective way of changing relationships than verbal exploration or discussion. Some assessment must be made of the emotional state of each. Anxiety and anger can usually be readily recognized, as can suspicion, bitterness, even a sense of persecution. But sadness or depression can be readily concealed; apathy may be mistaken for detachment; emptiness, loneliness and despair may be overlain by a complexity of other affects. In this aspect of the assessment, the consultant has to take account of how the emotional state of one spouse affects the other and also how (s)he is affected by emotions expressed or otherwise. How the couple's emotions affect the consultant is an important source of evidence, given a sufficient sensitivity; it is also a guide to what the consultant may have to cope with in future sessions. Whether or not one or both has any kind of physical or mental handicap, and their state of physical health, may be important issues. While further response might have to be delayed until some physical illness has been treated, it may be that working towards a resolution of marital problems is the most significant contribution to the process of recovery.

Crucial to any decision about continuing work together is an assessment of what it is the couple seek to change or improve and whether or not they have the same agenda: 'I want our marriage to be better' is perhaps a beginning, but not enough for a commitment. To one 'I'd like us to talk more,' might for the other mean 'But that would mean we have to spend more time together.' So is their view of how they think they might go about resolving their problems: 'Talking's no good, we need to *do* something' is not an uncommon view. Questions of motivation are often discussed in terms of whether spouses express the wish to change, have a desire for some kind of betterment in their life together, have the capacity or determination to put time and energy into creating that new state. These need also to be associated with questions of purpose, the purposes which the problems indicate and express and which may have to be greatly modified if overt wishes are to be achieved. 'My God, if she stops being tired, you'll be the first to wake her up' or 'If I have to stop seeing my friend I'll have to leave my husband.' A particular purpose which requires exploration is whether the search for help is a means towards some kind of reconciliation, resolution, or a step towards separation. A couple may say they wish to stay married, or to separate, but that apparent agreement often quickly turns out to be not so. Or a couple may seek help as a way of finding an answer to their ambivalence about staying together. Or the possibility of regularly meeting with an outsider, an 'expert', particularly someone described as therapist, may serve indefinitely to postpone the day of decision. Lest we forget: 'If you think you can get *us* to agree, you'd better chair the next East-West summit,' as one wife said.

In deciding *how best to respond*, practitioners have no right to assume that couples understand the nature of therapy, counselling, consultation. It cannot be assumed that they know what it would involve for them. Even less can they be expected to know that what is on offer might be constrained by a limitation on the consultant's skills or by matters of policy in the organization of which the consultant is a member. It is necessary therefore that in making an offer to work together with the couple, the consultant must give enough information about him/herself, methods of working, the employing or supporting organization, to help the couple make a decision. Alternatively, if no offer is to be made, the consultant should explain why and should be clear whether, in these circumstances, responsibilities include a recommendation about, or referral to, another practitioner. Our offer would be one of further consultation, of being available as a resource to assist the couple in the resolution of their problems. This is not to say that treatment is not recommended. One, possibly both spouses, may have a condition which requires treatment and the problem is then in deciding whether that is an alternative or an accompaniment to consultation or a necessary preliminary; for example, it seemed inappropriate to begin regular consultations with a couple until the husband's severely manic-depressive condition had been brought under control by medication. In another case, continuing work did not seem contraindicated where the wife was severely anxious and the husband on medication for high blood pressure after a myocardial infarction ('heart attack'). But the need for each individual to have treatment seemed paramount in the case of a wife whose life was dominated by obsessional compulsions and rituals and her husband whose schizophrenic condition had already twice become psychotic. If further consultation is to be offered, then in our view, that must be to the couple, the expectation being that they will attend *together* and that the focus will be on their relationship. All the available evidence points to this pattern as the most likely to be effective. Practitioners have to decide the conditions under which they will accept that only one spouse can or will attend:

is this is to be done then still the focus should be on the relationship rather than primarily on the experiences and intrapsychic life of the person attending. Working with couples in couple groups is an alternative known to be effective for some couples, but currently not widely practised.

Whether or not to offer help is rarely a simple issue and not one about which we can easily lay down ground rules. There are a variety of issues here which affect individual practitioners and the statutory or voluntary agencies to which they belong. Some psychiatrists would say that their priority is to treat people who are ill, not to offer help to those with problems in their relationships. Some counsellors say that they should not offer counselling to anyone who appears to be severely depressed, seeing this state always as an illness. Social workers faced with increasing demands and major crises in family life may have neither the priority, nor the time, nor the skills to focus especially on marital problems. General practitioners say their time is limited, and their training inadequate. Nor can we yet, with confidence, answer such a fundamental question as: what methods are most likely to be helpful in resolving what kind of problems presented by particular types of couple? Some so-called contraindications to further intervention are stated with unjustified authority. While couples in different age groups may present problems appropriate to their age and stage of development, the duration of their relationship, their age as such, is no contraindication, especially not 'elderliness'. Those described as verbally inarticulate, poorly educated, socially disadvantaged, part of so-called 'multiproblem families' should not for these reasons be seen as unlikely to respond: experience shows that such couples may greatly benefit from consultation. They can develop increased capacity to communicate effectively with each other and with people outside the family; they can become more skilful at working through difficulties; they can become more confident in challenging or modifying adverse social and economic conditions. How much to offer, what time, effort, skills to commit to further work will depend on what is negotiated with the couple. A general principle might be that of minimum effective intervention, that is, what methods, what approaches can be effective while being economic of time and what changes can be initiated which will enable the couple to continue on their own without the assistance of the consultant? An offer of further consultation must be provisional, because what it means and involves must be discussed with the couple; it is a basis for negotiation, for the triad to work together towards a decision. This can be a complex, difficult and sometimes prolonged process, which may not be complete by the end of the first consultation and which may require renegotiation and redefinition at later stages of the process.

Consultant and couple must reach some kind of agreement about the *aims of further meetings*. In this the consultant has a responsibility greater than that of the couple, given that experience and competence will be guides to what is possible, what is attainable. Possibilities will range from relief or amelioration of distress, to radical change. At the very least, though this may turn out to be a great deal, aims should be concerned with enlarging the couple's capacity to communicate with each other in an effective way and with learning jointly to resolve problems in ways which are mutually rewarding and which will maintain that process. In principle, the consultant should have in mind that aims should be specific rather than general; potentially attainable rather than the expression of some vague, benign hope and within the capacity of the consultant as well as that of the spouses. It is realistic that aims should be partial rather than global; relatively short term rather than for a lifetime and that they should be subject to review as incremental gains are made.

There is room and need for negotiation about aims, but there is a fundamental existential question to be considered with the majority of couples who seek help. This is concerned with how best to assist each of two more or less mature, more or less independent, adults to find and maintain an acceptable identity and sense of difference, within a long-term stable relationship. Further, the question addresses the dilemma of whether and how the relationship can provide, at one and the same time, a mutually sufficient degree of closeness and intimacy and a mutually acceptable degree of space or distance. These are in our view, considerations which apply to all marital work. These existential realities cannot properly be seen in terms of treatment of illness, though their resolution might be regarded as the ultimate aim of intervention. That would be a major commitment, because it seems to us possible that a resolution of this need, conflict and paradox is the ultimate task and purpose of marriage. Negotiating a programme for continuing intervention will include consideration of the frequency, timing and duration of sessions. Details are a matter for particular circumstances and cases: here we wish simply to assert that these decisions should depend less on a general rule, for example that all couples must be seen weekly, monthly or whatever, and more on an exploration of what seems practical and realistic for a particular couple and consultant.

There has been much talk in recent years about the need to define and agree a *contract* with the couple. This can be used in a limiting way to imply that only particular issues will be focused on, or will be dealt with only in particular ways; and it can be seen as having a binding quality, equivalent to a legal contract, often a means of trying to ensure commitment (usually it is the couple's commitment, not the consultant's, which is thought to require confirmation). The terms 'contract', 'commitment' and 'covenant' are used in relation to the promise made in public at the time of marriage. While it would be unwise to invest the consultant with the role of priest or registrar, these terms which describe and define agreement, have many layers of meaning and in that sense reflect the reality of decisions which can be reached.

Ending a consultation, especially the first, is an important process. Preferably it should finish within the time set aside and not be allowed to drift to an end, or be terminated because the consultant has no further time. The end of the first consultation may herald the closure of any relationship between husband, wife and practitioner. But it may be a transition between the assessment of a problem presented and the beginning of them working together towards change. Whatever the reality, it needs to be managed with as much sensitivity as the beginning.

CONTENT AND PROCESS IN CONSULTING TOGETHER WITH COUPLES

We shall, as in earlier sections, talk of the consultant in the singular, that is, we are not offering a model for co-consultation, either of the arrangement whereby two practitioners are together with the couple at the same time, or another in which practitioners work separately with the spouses. We concentrate on the triadic arrangement, because there is no evidence that other forms are more effective and the use of one rather than two consultants per couple is evidently more economic in staff terms. Nor shall we be discussing work with couples in groups: Skynner (1980) and James and Wilson (1986) clearly demonstrate the importance and value of marital group therapy, but we have no experience of applying the consultative model in group settings. Our exposition is about being a consultant to couples, of being available as a resource to them in their search for a resolution and helping them to use that resource. It is also about working together with couples, of joining with them in a collaborative venture. It is not always easy to differentiate clearly between responsibility, role, technique, task and focus, so that in using some of these terms we have recognized overlap.

We have already described a major *responsibility* of the consultant: to create and manage the setting in the interests of the work to be done. Related to this is the responsibility to create an environment in which that which is fearful or destructive can be held and contained; in which mutuality and reciprocity can become features of the engagement. The consultant's mode of working will to an important degree determine how quickly can be established a culture in which the three can find a language which all can use, and themes which can command and hold attention. For all consultants confidentiality is a matter of first priority, though our experience is that for most couples this is not a central concern. Most couples seem to take it for granted that consultants will not wish to discuss their problem with other people unless this is considered to be in the couple's interest. Most are surprised when care is taken to ensure that consent to any form of disclosure is discussed and fully granted. This trust, so often readily given, is a great privilege. A negative consequence of its importance is that for some practitioners it has constrained their willingness to accept consultation or supervision or to participate in evaluation of their work. Occasionally, one or both spouses will insist that no written record be kept, or that particular information be excluded. The consultant must discuss the reasons for this and the consequences and also accept responsibility for whatever he or she decides. A spouse, seen alone, may request that information be withheld from the other: as one wife said, 'You must of course feel free when you see my husband, to refer if you want, to our talk. You know I trust you to do as you think best. But you do not have my permission to mention my relationship with Gavin. That would be too much for Jack (the husband). So it must remain a secret between us.' It is not wise to accept restrictions like this and the working through of why might mean that there are no further consultations. Similarly, it is not wise to accept responsibility for conveying information from one spouse to the other, especially as ways can usually be found to help the spouse to do this for himself or herself.

There is some value in each of the two apparently contradictory statements about the *roles* of consultant: 'Don't just sit there, do something,' is a warning against passivity and a reminder of responsibility; 'You don't have to keep doing things, just be there,' is a warning that active intervention can at times become inappropriate (and unhelpful) interference. Consultants have a series of roles which may be seen as in conflict or as complementary or as a necessary paradox which mirrors some of the realities of the marital relationship. The practitioner must be discrete from the system which is the couple relationship, while at the same time being one of a triad, open to this experience and able to use it in the service of the work. The consultant needs to observe and think and be monitoring the impact of the experience, all at the same time. To be an insider, while holding in the mind the realities of outside worlds; to focus on the immediate present, while appreciating this in the context of the past and of possible futures: these are complex roles.

The consultant is, in a number of senses, a mirror. A couple may come to view themselves by the ways in which the consultant responds to them, because they will assume that the response is particular and specific to them. The consultant, in the mutual process of exploring problems, will reflect back what is being said as a way of affirming and defining it, of ensuring that each spouse knows what is being said. Another kind of mirroring, but potentially negative in its consequence, is the reflecting back of problems which originate in the consultant. This kind of process may express something of the consultant's life and past or it may be as it were brought in from the consultant's professional world or agency or service – in which one can so readily observe the interpersonal and institutional problems which also characterize the institution of marriage (a theme to which we shall return in part 4). In such a consultation, with three people in the room, only two can at any one time communicate effectively – when all three speak at once it can be funny, but it can also be very distressing and may impede the process. When two persons are intensely engaged with each other in the presence of a third, that third can have a variety of experiences. The person may take on or become caught up in one (or more) of several roles, as the observer, or the excluded one, or the interloper. To be outside the pair can be the role of husband, wife, consultant, and that may change many times throughout a consultation. In these terms a major aim of the consultative process is that husband and wife talk to each other. The consultant's role is to be able to expand and deepen their discourse, with a reduction in fear or anger or conflict. But for a time husband and wife may be able to talk to each other only through the consultant. Being such a third can be a difficult role, an uncomfortable experience; but from its nature the consultant can learn something of what is difficult for each spouse, of what is needed and wanted, of what it can feel like to be the object of attack or suspicion, or attachment, or dependence.

Such a role, as transference object or transitional object (Haldane and McCluskey 1982), an essentially empathic position, can be used to help husband and wife relate to each other's experience. While in one-to-one psychotherapy it may be seen as essential to the process that the therapist interpret transference/counter-transference phenomena, i.e. features of the patient-therapist relationship echoed in past and other current relationships), this is not so central a task in work with couples. The priority is to explore and identify with husband and wife the ways in which other past or current relationships determine or colour their own; how each can be perceived and experienced, not so much as the person he or she is, as the kind of person the spouse needs him or her to be, or the person with whom the spouse has not yet worked out problems and conflicts recurring from the past. A central task for the consultant may be to help husband and wife learn who and what the other person is in reality *now* and to use that learning as a basis on which to build a relationship for the future. Of course, such a process carries the risk that a discovery or rediscovery of reality may not be tolerable or acceptable. For some spouses, a discovery of what the other is 'really like' may come as a shock and for others as a confirmation of what was already dimly perceived. And the same may apply to learning about oneself. What to do with such learning demands choices and stimulates challenge. The results range from a confirmation of mutual satisfactions, aspirations and values in the relationship as an exciting basis for the future, to a confirmation of that which has been feared or suspected and the realization that dissolution of the relationship is for each the only hope of finding an acceptable sense of self and freedom to mature on the basis of that discovery. As one husband said: 'There's no marks to be gained for what we've learned about ourselves, only pain at the moment and some hope for the future.'

The consultant *manages* the boundaries of time and space, acting as a protector who ensures against intrusion and who sees that the sessions have a clear beginning and end. This means managing the zones of space, time, experience, which husband and wife, each in their individual way, cross as they enter and leave the consultation, a crossing or transition which has to be managed supportively and with delicacy. One may see these transitions in simple terms, such as giving husband and wife time to settle down, get used to the surroundings again, shift the focus of their awareness, or as allowing time for them to be ready to leave, gather themselves together, be ready for whatever everyday task awaits them. But these movements in and out of the framework of consultation have parallels in the ways in which each spouse has constantly to make the transition between their own inner life and the worlds of persons in which they live, between the world say of idealization and reality, between the realities of their relationship and the social, public world. From how these transactions are managed, husband and wife may learn to organize time and attention and space as priority for themselves, how they can remain aware of, yet not feel assaulted by, the expectations and intentions of what is outside the immediacy of their relationship – children, friends, other interests, society's quarrels about what is good or bad, healthy or sick, within marriage. There are also boundaries between conscious and unconscious life, between self and other, between one particular marriage and others. In health one state of being is not overwhelmed by the other, the boundaries which help to define identity are clear; interchange, interaction, can take place between one and the other. To some extent, who and what we are is contributed to by the introjections and projections which belong to our experiences with others. It may be a role of the consultant to help husband and wife be so sufficiently freed from these effects as to feel free in themselves, less burdened by emotions or conflicts which more appropriately are part of the other. In this boundary-keeping function, the consultant is in a position of potential power and control, in influencing the kind of information which crosses a boundary, for example he/she may with confidence be aware of what one spouse feels but cannot express about the other and so can (indeed must) choose whether to promote such expression or leave it be. The problems experienced in the relationship may replicate those currently being expressed in public debate, for example gender roles, the normality of particular sexual behaviours, control of money. The public debate may be easier to talk about than it is to explore each spouse's contributions to their own problems. The private and the public territory needs to be kept separate, yet ways need to be found to relate each to the other; to see how one influences and reflects the other, while using such an understanding primarily in the service of resolving the couple's problems. To hold to or perhaps to redefine clear boundaries is to differentiate between what is on each side. That redefinition must not be achieved at the expense of rigidity in the boundary systems or of an incapacity to allow transaction and to learn from interchange. It is one aspect of holding the paradox, of maintaining the creative differences which might otherwise be destructive.

The primary *focus* of work with couples, that which should determine all aspects of the intervention, is their relationship: the ways in which each experiences, thinks about, reacts towards the other; the emotional states, behaviours, level and nature of communication characteristic of their interaction; that which holds them together, maintains their particular relationship, whether experienced as bonds of affectionate attachment or as restraining, constricting binds.

A range of methods and techniques is available to assist and encourage husband and wife to explore and find meaning in their problems. As we indicated earlier, the most basic is attentive listening, not only to the couple by the consultant, but also by each spouse towards the other. After listening, talking: to help husband and wife to talk to each other in ways which are pleasing, positive and productive rather than painful and destructive is at once a method or technique and also an aim which should have a high priority. It may take a long time to achieve this and it is rarely done easily. If a spouse shouts, accuses, does so at great length and in detail, the other will, at the very least, stop listening. To interrupt an angry tirade or prolonged tears is neither easy nor simple: the first can result in one becoming the object of an attack and the second in distressed observations about one's lack of sensitivity. Consultant: 'Mr H., how do you think your wife experiences what you have said?' Husband: 'Who asked you to interrupt!' Or consultant: 'Mrs A., I'm wondering how your husband reacts to your tears.' Wife: 'I thought you at least would be sensitive. All you do is take his side.' Just as consultants need to keep their interventions brief and not indulge in prolonged statements, so they need to help husband and wife not to make speeches at each other, to engage in a dialogue where each can make frequent contributions.

The more husband and wife can talk to and with each other, the more able they will be to explore their problems and ways of resolving them; to tease out, disentangle the complexity of the problems and find that there are steps and stages in their resolution, rather than that solutions can be achieved in one great leap. It is facile, in the sense of both easy and superficial, to think of a straightforward process of finding simple solutions. Few couples welcome this: they have already tried that tack and failed. These steps towards a possible resolution involve continuing negotiation, trial and error, success and failure. If handled with concern and patience it can result in the hitherto unspeakable being said and heard. And what is unspeakable will be different for different persons. Wife to husband: 'I've wished you dead since Joan (the youngest child) was born.' Husband to wife: 'We've never had sex without me imagining that you were someone else.' Wife, of her extramarital relationship, to husband: 'Yes, we've been sleeping together, no, not just this year, for ten years.'

Exploring and identifying the history of problems and the relevance of this process to the present, can be helped by asking the couple to list, chronologically, events or experiences which have in some way been important in their lives both before and after marriage. They can do so in the presence of the consultant or at home, each on their own, or together. Such lists are then reviewed in order to discover the meaning of events for each spouse, the differences in interpretation, the assumptions each has about the importance for the other. With many couples there is an awareness, more or less conscious, that their problems are in some senses a repetition of those experienced by parents, or similar to those current in other members of the extended family. And it is often the case that the family marital problem which one spouse accuses the other of having brought into the marriage is equally or more evident in his or her own family. Couples can be helped to review factual information about each other's family as well as to explore the myths each entertains about their own and the other's family, by drawing out a detailed family tree or geneogram, being encouraged to talk about their discoveries, being helped to appreciate the relevance of history and other people's relationships to their own and in turn being freed from the past, able to leave it behind.

Consultation cannot be practised simply by following a set of rules or procedures but there are some *attitudes or actions to be avoided*, so we offer these guidelines for practice. Too much talk can prevent communication: listen attentively and do not interrupt unless you need to and know why. Eliciting information is not an interrogation, so try to keep it relaxed. Keep to the point, be brief and do not lecture. Social chat, however well intended, is not what couples come for. It is not helpful to apportion blame, to referee or adjudicate: whatever the couple feel, this is not a trial. Often accused and accuser are present, but the role of counsel for prosecution or defence, however excitingly attractive, does not belong to consultations. Being judge or jury can be even more seductive but is equally to be avoided. Reassurance is likely to be only temporarily helpful and is often misjudged. It is rarely helpful to tell a husband and wife that one has dealt with similar problems, even worse to observe that their problems are less severe than they had thought and no consolation to make it clear that one's expertise arises from having overcome similar problems in one's own marriage. No matter how competent and however justified your confidence, avoid giving advice about how best to resolve the problems: at the least this will be ignored, it may be resisted and it may offer yet further ground for a husband and wife anti-consultant alliance. The 'if onlys' and other aspects of the past, may be interesting, even important in understanding the present, but to focus too much on the past can become no more than an endlessly fascinating diversion for all three. However much husband and wife are responsible for what they do and become, try not to let them get into irreversible positions of confrontation or defence, even though one may be thus deprived of the satisfactions of helping them solve such an impasse. Especially try not to be clever; and avoid scoring points. To try to take away the emotional distress being experienced by husband and wife, in some way to relieve them of that burden, is to deprive them of an existential resource in their search for resolution.

That couples, no less than individuals or families, find difficulty in altering behaviour, or experience of others, or the nature of relationships, is a fact of experience. Such difficulty in change may be determined by one or more individuals in the triad of consultation, or by factors in the wider family and social context. One may construe these difficulties in terms of resistance (Rycroft 1972) or 'stuckness' (Treacher 1985) but one must constantly keep in mind that the lack of change, or insufficient change, may be explained by the consultant's limitations or incompetence. The psychoanalytic concept of resistance is complex, many-layered, descriptive and non-judgemental; it has too readily become a kind of critical comment, a view of patient or client behaviour which implies a positive resistance to or an active rebellion against the kind of change sought by therapist, counsellor, consultant. Such a pejorative view results in struggles for power, each side needing to win. If the consultant becomes caught up in such a struggle, so too might the spouses in relation to each other. A recognition that an overt wish for change may be accompanied by an unrecognized determination to maintain the status quo should be a call to patience and empathy rather than to developing strategies for winning. A technical problem for the consultant who works with couples, as for those who work with families, is that the constituent individuals of the system are likely to be different in their desire and capacity for change and the rate of change which it is possible for them to tolerate. That difference is, of course, grist to the mill of assisting couples to explore their idiosyncrasies and particularities; to assess and allow for their probably disparate needs and to distinguish their capacities to develop and mature.

Sessions must end, preferably on time, and so must programmes of intervention, hopefully with husband and wife able to continue the resolving of problems with increased resources and confidence. How to end, how to make the transition from an institutionalized form of helping to living out the problems in the world outside the boundaries of the consultation, is not and should not be a simple, routine exercise. One may agree with the couple that time should define the boundary, in which case one must close even at a time of tension, conflict, lack of resolution. Or one may agree to use the last period of the session for review of what has been learned, what might be continued, what yet needs to be attended to. But no session and no programme of consultation can be complete in the sense of all problems being resolved or of final resolutions being achieved. Life remains to be lived, and husband and wife have to do so together, without intervention, without the presence of a third person.

The experience of this kind of consultation is at the least interesting and nearly always complex. It can be distressing, because couples can bring problems which are painful, long term and overwhelming. It can be daunting and disturbing, couple by couple, and knowing that these husbands and wives represent only a small proportion of those who might seek some kind of relief. It can be perplexing and confusing, exasperating when couples demonstrate their expertise, despite all one's efforts, at maintaining stalemate. Feelings of pleasure and achievement are a bonus, often unexpected or unanticipated. Sometimes the experience can be fun, because some husbands and wives, against all the odds, retain some sense of humour, so that laughter becomes a remembered sharing.

Our focus in part 3 has been on husbands and wives in relationship and on the transactions which take place when couples meet with consultants. However professionally conducted, these encounters are always private and personal; but they also have their public, organizational dimensions which influence the various ways in which couples and consultants may come together. It is to some of these influences that we now turn in part 4.

4

The Organizational Context of Research and Intervention

In this part of the book we shall go on to examine a number of issues concerning the history, development and current state of practice, training and research in marital work. In doing this we shall have a good deal to say, much of which is critical, about the organizational context in which such work is conducted.

The fullest discussion of the interrelationships between practice, training and research in this field is still to be found in *Marriage Matters*, the consultative document on marriage guidance produced by a Home Office working party in consultation with the Department of Health and Social Security, and published in 1979. Though the report produced comment in the medical journals at the time (*BMJ* 1979), it was several years before Morgan (1985) published a rather fuller discussion of its recommendations and underlying philosophy. For Morgan, a fundamental problem of *Marriage Matters* is its tendency to assume a particularly narrow interpretation of marriage as *relationship*, defined primarily in terms of its private, interpersonal dimensions. This analysis, he argues, gives little prominence to marriage as a public *institution*, intricately connected to wider social structures and processes. We would agree with this. What we find more difficult to accept however is Morgan's argument that *Marriage Matters'* attempt to develop recommendations for the integration of research and practice in marital work leads it inevitably to a 'medical model' of marriage which 'remains supreme' (Morgan 1985:31). We would contend that there are indeed possibilities for such an integration, between research and practice, which contrary to Morgan's rather pessimistic viewpoint, can allow the voices of history, sociology and phenomenology to be heard. In an earlier phase of working together, in our then roles of social researcher and university teacher/

practitioner, we learned that each could benefit from the other's corpus of knowledge and practice. Later, when we were involved in the management of a marriage counselling service, the need for the integration of evaluation and research with practice and training became even more evident and pressing. Equally clear however was that this could not be achieved unless accompanied by an understanding and modification of the *organizational* context in which collaborative work might take place.

Regrettably, there has been no response to the proposal in *Marriage Matters* for regional units in which practice, training and research would be the integrated remit of multidisciplinary teams. Only the Tavistock Institute of Marital Studies, over a period of 40 years, has significantly developed this pattern of work, in which staff contribute to all three areas of activity. Elsewhere, in research units, university and polytechnic departments, clinics and voluntary organizations, there have been few sustained efforts at integration. This may itself reflect the failure of *Marriage Matters* adequately to capture and anticipate the changing discourse of marriage in our society. The report exudes a certain hubris about counselling and intervention in personal relationships; a belief that unsatisfactory relationships not only can, but should, be improved by the use of skilled helpers. As we have shown in part 2, the social dimensions of marriage and marital problems are so complex that such a simple and optimistic view will inevitably be called into question. In particular, any approach to practice will have to take into account issues of gender and social class as important determinants of marital experience. *Marriage Matters* not only failed to recognize these complexities, but was also ill timed in relation to the changing social, political and ideological context of the period which followed. This included, on the one hand, a growing feminist discourse on marriage and, on the other, the assertions of some New Right commentators that the family has its own self-regulatory mechanisms which render unnecessary any interventions into its internal affairs.

Recognizing these constraints, we nevertheless still have confidence in a model which emphasizes the integration of perspectives in marital work. We believe that practice should be better informed by research and by evaluation. In turn research must focus more actively at times on the concerns of practitioners, enhancing the development of knowledge and skills, and carefully grounding clients' experiences in their social contexts. As we examine these related dimensions of marital work and marriage research, we shall therefore keep in mind the search for an organizational system in which they can develop in active, collaborative partnership.

Any organization, agency, unit or department which aims to offer marital counselling, therapy, consultation or research must be clear to a sufficient degree about its aims and objectives. This means being clear about priorities and the resources which are required to achieve and maintain an appropriate level of activity. However well these are defined and agreed, their achievement is dependent also on clarity about priorities in the work and the resources of personnel, finance and material necessary to maintain activity appropriate to the aims. Systems of responsibility and accountability have to be understood and seen to be implemented, if tasks are to be achieved and the organization's work reviewed and evaluated. Putting these principles into practice requires attention also to the organization's boundary, that imaginative perimeter which we discussed in part 3 in relation to the couple-consultant system, which helps define the organization's identity. In turn such identification will clarify differences and similarities with other organizations and facilitate interactions with them. These principles will particularly affect practice, training and research in organizations which undertake two or more of these activities.

It is possible to elaborate and define such principles in considerable detail, but definitions of this sort are then at risk of becoming rigid rules which are expected to cover or anticipate every contingency. It is preferable instead that they be subject to regular review, allowing flexibility and the possibility of development. If these principles for development are to be effectively defined in practice, it is essential that an organization's members and staff should share sufficient understanding and agreement about its *modus operandi*. We use the term 'sufficient' to mean that members or staff should be free to use their skills, while keeping to a minimum the time and energy required to administer and organize the system. This is not to say that administration and management do not matter, but to emphasize that their purpose is to promote the task of the organization: practice, training or research, or all of these. There is however a particularly important way in which orientation to the primary task may be disturbed.

We have already explained in part 3 that one of the skills of the consultant, counsellor or therapist is sometimes to 'reflect back' to an individual, couple or group some aspect of what they have done or said or seem to have experienced. This reflecting back may be as it were an echo or a reminder, or a note of what has been said, so that the speaker may hear it again or appreciate how it affected another. So something may be mirrored or repeated after consideration, transmuted by the observation or experience of the consultant. But there is also another sense in which individuals functioning as members of organizations may 'reflect back'. In doing so they convey to a greater or lesser degree, in simple or complicated ways, the dynamics of their organization: the tensions, conflicts, unresolved issues in which they are involved. This kind of 'reflecting back' may show the counsellors, therapists, researchers, individually or collectively behaving like the couples they see in their work. The more complex, conflictual, disturbed the relationships which are presented to the organization, the more the workers will have to attend to problems within their work with one another which show behaviour or experiences similar to those of the 'client' couples. It will be clear that the reflection process can be perceived as positive, helpful, enabling; or as negative, obstructive, disabling. However experienced, it can be the basis for learning and understanding, and this potential needs to be kept constantly in mind. Mattinson and Sinclair's (1979) study of marital work in a local authority social services department is a detailed and thorough demonstration of such dynamics.

These organizational problems are not rare. They will always exist to some degree. But their existence is often not appreciated, or is minimized and denied. There is therefore a constant risk that services or agencies concerned primarily to help persons resolve problems in relationships spend considerable effort and resources attending to personal and relationship conflicts among their own members, resulting in a reduction in the energies available to pursue the primary task in an effective way. These potential problems are inherent in the dynamics of a wide range of organizations.

4.1 Issues in Practice

The proportion of couples who seek help for problems in marriage is unknown. As we saw in part 2, we have little data on the prevalence of 'marital problems', however they are to be defined. When in difficulties, some couples may turn to friends, family or neighbours. We know that a certain proportion of individual spouses also look beyond these relatively private psychological territories to the more public domain of advice columnists and 'agony aunts'. Still others delve into the burgeoning literature on marital problems which is to be found in books and magazines; and in recent years a significant number of television broadcasts have also examined various aspects of marriage, family life, sexuality and personal relationships in ways which may be helpful to some persons. Beyond these varied, ad hoc and possibly limited forms of help, a certain proportion of couples may seek the help of one of the growing number of counsellors and therapists who practice privately and independently. Most couples however will need to negotiate entry into some kind of *organization* before any active helping response may begin. Achieving this can be a complex and difficult process and may require a considerable degree of both courage and persistence. Those who seek help in resolving their marital problems cannot easily find it in our society. For those who succeed, the process may be stressful and also may complicate the original problem.

It is by no means clear, even to specialists in the field, precisely which organizations offer help to couples. Whereas *Marriage Matters* advocated that 'many doors' should be available, in practice these are often poorly signposted or difficult to open. Likewise the report expressed the hope that those seeking help would find an adequate and competent response within any one of the agencies. This begs a number of questions, from how the services of such agencies are generally advertised and recognized within the community, to the extent to which their effectiveness can be evaluated. Recognizing that a detailed review of their work is well beyond the scope of this book, we briefly describe the agencies here before going on to raise some general issues about their activities.

THE MARRIAGE GUIDANCE COUNCILS

Even the most casual observer of the field of marital therapy and counselling in Britain would quickly note that the major source of help for couples is provided by the voluntary marriage guidance councils. This arrangement was first considered by the Harris committee of 1948 in its report on grants for the development of marriage guidance. Harris and his colleagues took the view that 'this is work which we believe is better left as far as possible to the initiative of the voluntary organisations and which cannot like other forms of social work be undertaken – at any rate at the present time and without further knowledge and experience – by official bodies' (HMSO 1948:9). Over the next 40 years this appears to have been the continuing viewpoint of successive governments; as we shall see, it has also remained a fairly accurate description of available services.

The first marriage guidance councils in England were formed in the late 1930s; the Catholic Marriage Advisory Council started in 1946; the Scottish Marriage Guidance Council and the Jewish Marriage Education Committee began in 1948. We shall concentrate here mainly on the work of the National Marriage Guidance Council (NMGC) for England, Wales and Northern Ireland and the Scottish Marriage Guidance Council (SMGC), which though separate organizations, share a number of features in common and are the major secular sources of marriage counselling in the United Kingdom. Both organizations have undergone significant changes since the mid-1980s; we were ourselves actively involved in these in the case of the SMGC.

The NMGC and the SMGC are federally structured organizations, with a central policy-making body linked to a network of relatively autonomous local branches. In 1986–7 there were 157 local marriage guidance councils (now known as Relate centres) in the NMGC and 15 in the SMGC. The branches run their own affairs, finding funding from local authorities, trusts, industry and from client donations. They must recruit counsellors and administrative workers, maintain adequate accommodation and promote the council's work within the community. In the NMGC there are minimum criteria for membership, which all councils must maintain; nevertheless, as in Scotland, where no such criteria apply, there are large variations between councils in different areas. Some marriage guidance councils, particularly those in the major cities, have large volunteer work forces of counsellors and receptionists and operate in their own premises, which are either leased or purchased. Elsewhere, particularly in rural areas, local councils may have a much more hand-to-mouth existence; premises may be shared with other voluntary or statutory services; the number of counsellors may be low and a variety of problems may result from inadequate funding and limited public interest or support. In some cases these inequities between councils may mirror other broader trends within the country as a whole. For example data collected by the NMGC on the financial contributions made by clients to assist in the cost of their counselling shows highest averages in the South East of the country, with lowest receipts in the North West.

The amount of counselling undertaken by the marriage guidance councils has been steadily increasing, though growth has been more limited in Scotland. In 1986–7 the NMGC opened over 45,000 new 'cases' and conducted a total of 251,500 interviews; the SMGC (serving a population approximately one-tenth the size) opened 2,633 new cases and carried out 11,268 interviews. Less than one-fifth of all interviews are carried out with male clients alone, with the remainder equally split between lone female clients and couples. They were seen by volunteer counsellors who number 1,800 in the NMGC and 140 in the SMGC. Those wishing to become counsellors are recruited locally, through a pre-selection process, known as sponsoring; they are then subjected to a full selection procedure which has been developed and is administered by the national organization using both paid staff and external selectors. Over a considerable period of time in both organizations, and despite the fact that their selection procedures vary somewhat, a fairly constant acceptance rate of 50 per cent has been maintained. Each organization has its own nationally organized training programme in which its volunteers must take part and also agree to be available for a minimum of 120 hours of counselling per year.

In both the NMGC and the SMGC the initial counsellor training programme lasts for two years and includes residential sessions. Both programmes have undergone considerable change and development in recent years, and the NMGC has introduced a modular approach, which integrates experiential work with technical skills and an appreciation of theoretical issues. Each counsellor is allocated to a tutor who takes responsibility with the counsellor for his or her development through the initial training and beyond. Counsellors also attend local case discussion groups, led by tutors or others from outside the organization, many of whom have particular expertise in marital work. Tutors are employed part-time on a sessional basis by the national organization.

Both organizations have a relatively small staff at national level and have struggled in recent years to undertake developments consistent with both growing demands on the service and broader social changes in patterns of marriage formation and dissolution. This however is in part a reflection of the levels of central government grant aid which have been made available. In 1986–7 the NMGC received a Home Office grant of £890,000, accounting for almost 60 per cent of its income; the SMGC received a total of £58,000 from the Scottish Education Department, representing some 68 per cent of its total income for that year. Both organizations have repeatedly complained of the inadequacies of these awards but in recent years, despite incremental improvements, they have failed to achieve the exponential rise in grant aid which they have consistently sought. It would be a great mistake however to imagine that the problems of the two major voluntary marriage counselling organizations have been entirely financial.

The founders of the marriage guidance movement in Britain were clear about their task. Alarmed by rising trends in divorce, their goal was to save marriages from breakdown and in so doing limit the resultant personal and social damage. In the early years marriage guidance was about 'marriage mending' and its claims to moral and financial support were made unequivocally on that basis. However, as the public and professional discourse around divorce began to alter during the 1960s and increasingly in the 1970s, such a position became difficult to maintain. A growing number of commentators began to see divorce as the manifestation of free choice on the part of adults who should not be constrained, morally or legally, to remain in marriages which were unhappy and even detrimental to the health and wellbeing of themselves and their children. The marriage guidance councils found themselves with the problem of deciding to what extent they should accommodate to this changing social climate. Already the emphasis of the work had shifted away from the concept of *guidance* in favour of *counselling*, essentially in a 'person-centred' mode derived from the work of Carl Rogers in the United States. This reflected a desire to offer non-judgemental, unconditional regard for clients, rather than some form of prescriptive advice.

By the mid-1970s therefore the journal *Marriage Guidance* contains numerous articles devoted to the question of the organization's *primary task*, and this process of reflection and review eventually led to the formation of the working party which produced *Marriage Matters*. Indeed it is interesting to note that the working party was not so much a product of governmental concern about the work of the marital agencies, but rather a result of preoccupations and anxieties developing within the agencies themselves, which were drawn to the attention of somewhat unwilling officials. That is certainly a reasonable conclusion to draw from subsequent governmental indifference to the report, coupled with continuing organizational uncertainties.

Part of this concern about the primary task resulted from a growing diversity in the work undertaken by the marriage guidance councils. In addition to the core programme of selecting and training counsellors for work in the local groups, resources were also being allocated to areas of development, such as sex therapy, education work, research, publishing and the provision of training to other agencies and professional groups. Such developments were difficult to fund and inevitably raised questions about the most effective use of limited resources. Was 'prevention better than cure', for example, in the proposal that greater attention should be given to work with young people and those about to be married; and, if so, precisely what sort of images and values about marriage should be promoted? In some parts of the organization research was no more a priority then than now; practice seems so much more important than evaluation, experiencing more valuable than knowing, doing more worthwhile than thinking. Sex therapy, on the other hand, forced a consideration of the wider agenda of sexuality and changing sexual mores in our society, recognizing not least that some clients were coming for help who were not married to one another and who may indeed be in homosexual rather than heterosexual relationships. It is interesting that the NMGC still refers to this aspect of its work as *marital* sexual therapy.

These and a variety of other considerations, which we cannot explore in detail here, caused considerable tensions and differences, particularly within the NMGC. We have found a thoughtful article by Chester (1985a) very useful in making some sense of these processes, tensions and conflicts. Chester suggests that they should be seen as aspects of organizational change whereby the NMGC (but the same principles would also apply to the SMGC) has developed from a *movement* into an *agency*. By this is implied a process wherein a broadly based, relatively diffuse, structurally underdeveloped social movement, held together by a loose belief system, develops into a managerially more complex, increasingly codified and bureaucratized service agency with rationally stated objectives and clearer systems of accountability. As Chester puts it: 'the former has *values* to promote and *members* to affirm them, whilst the latter has *objectives* to achieve and *personnel* to implement them' (1985a:6). At the heart of all this is the crucial transition from a movement broadly committed to the defence of marriage as an institution, to an increasingly specialized agency dedicated to the treatment of marital and other relationship problems. This shift, of course, exactly mirrors the changing dis-course of marriage, which we explored in part 2, from *institution* to *relationship*.

Both the NMGC and the SMGC have explicitly recognized the implications of this transition. In 1986 the NMGC commissioned management consultants to undertake a major review, with recom-mendations, of the organization's aims, management structure, fund-ing, public image and technical services. Adopted by its council later that year, the report produced sweeping changes, in headquarters staff, in national and regional management structure and in particular in approaches to the growing financial strictures which have affected the council. The management consultants concluded that 'the option of carrying on broadly as before, albeit with some fine-tuning of the present organization, would not be sustainable' (NMGC 1986:5). More limited, but reflecting the same concern for a fundamental review of the organization's activities, the SMGC adopted a Five-Year Plan of development in 1985, which concluded: 'Our organisation has no right to survival. It must be able to demonstrate its effectiveness to a variety of audiences if its medium term future is to be secured' (SMGC 1986:33). This plan also brought about changes in management, staffing and financial control and led to a major examination of selection, training and the tutorial system. In 1986 the SMGC adopted a new set of aims, which abandoned any over-arching moral statement about marriage and the family in favour of a clear statement of organizational activities and objectives.

The most visible evidence of these changes can be seen in the NMGC's decision to adopt a new name, with effect from early 1988, a move timed to coincide with the organization's fiftieth anniversary. Although the registered name of 'marriage guidance' remains, both the national body and the local groups now operate on a day-to-day basis under the name 'Relate'. The new name was adopted on the advice of external public relations and marketing consultants. Such changes continue to underline the shift from movement to agency. The decision to adopt the new name of Relate, which has not been followed by the SMGC, reveals the increasing tendency to emphasize the interpersonal, *relational* aspects of marriage. Indeed, we take the view that the name not only throws into shadow the complex structural dimensions of marriage and partnership in our society, but that it emphasizes those interpersonal, private aspects in ways which may be unhelpful. As we attempt to show throughout this book, relationships between persons, and particularly those which take place inside the institution we call marriage, carry a heavy public script. If this is ignored, the most likely outcome will be the further frustration and disappointment of those who have been encouraged to see the interpersonal world as *tabula rasa*, upon which, once suitably empowered, they need only draw the scenario of their choice. In this sense 'relate' as either nomenclature or exhortation, recalls an earlier period, of the 1960s and 1970s, the flawed legacy of which, as we have seen, was *Marriage Matters*.

SOCIAL SERVICES DEPARTMENTS

Far less can be said with any confidence about the place of marital work within the domain of the statutory social services. *Marriage Matters* recognized that the capacity of social service departments to undertake this sort of work was exceedingly limited and that for a variety of reasons there had been a sharp decline in the amount of marital work undertaken by the probation service. On the one hand social work appears now increasingly concerned with crisis intervention of one sort or another, much of this being in the context of statutory responsibilities and welfare provision. And on the other there is the question of adequate training among social workers to undertake intensive work with couples. We believe that all workers in the caring professions, including social workers, require further training in order to carry out marital work effectively and responsibly; none of the current basic grade training programmes within the caring professions offer adequate training in marital work. Moreover, even for those social workers with further training, there are the organizational difficulties of securing permission to undertake the work and of being provided with appropriate supervision or consultation.

James and Wilson (1986) have produced a detailed discussion of the constraints which limit the practice of marital work in social services agencies. They also suggest ways forward, not least by emphasizing the importance of this kind of work within the full panoply of social services provision, and by offering encouragement to those interested to undertake it. But we note that these exhortations are pitched at the level of the individual worker, who may be relatively powerless in determining policies which could lead to the wider provision of marital counselling or therapy with couples. This is particularly depressing since James and Wilson and others (Mattinson and Sinclair 1979) recognize that social workers routinely encounter considerable numbers of cases in which, by whatever set of criteria are adopted, some form of marital problem may be said to exist. In some instances indeed marital problems may be at the very heart of those highly complex and long-standing cases which demand so much of a worker's time and of the agency's resources. Social workers may consciously or unconsciously avoid this component in their cases. In some situations they may refer the couple to one of the specialist agencies. It appears highly unlikely that many workers would be able to offer any sustained opportunity for the couple to work with their difficulties.

So we are left unable to say much from the available literature about the range, forms and extent of marital work carried out in social services departments. The picture is a rather depressing one, particularly as portrayed by Mattinson and Sinclair (1979), who, even in the context of a research project concerned with the specialized provision of experienced marital therapists to an inner London social services department on an experimental basis, found intractable difficulties. We know that their account has echoes for other social workers who have encountered the complexities of identifying marital problems in the context of an intricate web of personal and material problems presented by clients, and of then engaging with couples and maintaining a focus in ways which may be helpful. It also shows how 'the system' seems to conspire against the achievement of these tasks and how easy it is for all concerned, workers and clients, to collude in stalemate; each finding that someone else is to blame for the lack of progress. Almost in passing, James and Wilson tellingly summarize the constraints on marital work in the social services: 'worker anxiety and lack of confidence, organisational and statutory frameworks, and clients inhibition' (1986:98).

MEDICAL SETTINGS

It may therefore seem to be the case that, as far as the statutory services are concerned, the potential for marital work is greatest in medical settings: general practice, departments of psychiatry, units offering family therapy and so on. Again, we are unable here to present a comprehensive review, but a brief account of the contours of the landscape will show a situation which is both patchy and far from encouraging, at least to those who believe that sources of marriage counselling and marital therapy should be more easily and more widely available.

To talk about marital work in clinical settings is immediately to raise anxieties about the *medicalization* of marital problems, to which we have already referred. And we may well wish to ask why and to what extent help with difficulties in the relationship called marriage should be particularly forthcoming from those whose training has been principally medical and clinical. One reason for such a connection is undoubtedly due to the observable association between marital status and health. We have explored this in earlier sections and we have seen that an illness model may be the one most readily available to spouses when seeking somehow to define the nature of their unhappiness and present it to a third party. Here there may be a problem of recognition; as *Marriage Matters* noted in evidence presented by the Royal College of General Practitioners, 'Marital unhappiness can present as depression, as a headache or backache or a heavy period or a child who refuses to go to school' (*Marriage Matters* 1979:145). In these circumstances, the skill of the practitioner – and it may be a doctor, health visitor, district nurse, community psychiatric nurse or some other member of the primary care team – will be to 'hear' as well as listen, and by then reflecting back what has been heard give 'permission' to the patient to begin to define the issue in a more focused way. In this process medical practitioner and social worker share some options: to engage with the person and the presenting problem; to reframe the problem as something else (an illness or welfare issue); to respond as if no problem in relationship has been intimated; or to refer to a 'specialist' for counselling or therapy. In the context of primary care there is no way of knowing the magnitude of marital problems which present in this way, and we certainly are not in a position to suggest in what proportions the options are exercised. However, on the basis of the training currently offered to primary care workers there is little to suggest that many will be either motivated or sufficiently confident in their own skills to take on intensive work with couples.

A study by Lenn, carried out in Scotland in the 1970s, showed that marriage guidance counsellors found themselves more accepted and able to make working relationships in medical than in social settings (Lenn 1980). Subsequently there has been considerable growth, throughout Britain, in the numbers of marriage guidance counsellors practising in health centres and general practitioners' surgeries. This appears to be a fruitful initiative, though one marked by a number of clear difficulties, as demonstrated by the studies of Keithley (1982), de Groot (1985) and Corney (1986). Counsellors appear to enjoy working in this way, perhaps in part for the sense of status and professionalism which may go with the setting. A good deal will certainly depend upon the extent to which the counsellor can liaise effectively with the primary care team as a whole so that appropriate referrals can be made. This opportunity for direct referral is relatively uncommon in marriage guidance work in other settings; accordingly it has the potential to reduce waiting periods, and perhaps, as a result of the individual contacts within the health centre, give encouragement to couples or individual clients who are uncertain whether or not they wish to see a counsellor. On the other hand, problems of confidentiality may arise if medical information or details of the counselling are shared between the counsellor and the medical team. The counsellor's voluntary status may also create difficulties; counsellors will only be available on a limited time basis and there may be dissonances between their role in the practice and that of other paid staff. Perhaps most problematic of all is the tendency for marriage counsellors in medical settings to be deployed as *generic* counsellors, mainly seeing individual clients in connection with a wide range of personal and practial problems. This may ease the burdens of consultation for the general practitioner, but it will not promote a specific service in marital counselling to the patients. Given the counsellor's status ambiguity, it may be difficult to convince members of the primary care team of the need to maintain this sort of focus, particularly if they see some advantage to themselves in being able to pass 'difficult' patients to a willing listener.

While the recognition of marital problems in the primary care setting still allows work to be developed which is not disease orientated, elsewhere within the National Health Service, marital work in hospital outpatient clinics and psychiatric units may conform more narrowly to a medical model of intervention. At the very least it will be surrounded by an obvious aura of illness, treatment and cure; it will in most cases be conducted by doctors, though nurses and social workers may also be involved. It will be accompanied by the routines and institutional arrangements of hospital administration. Unless great efforts are made by staff, and these are likely to be heavily circumscribed by available resources, it is highly likely that 'patients' will perceive their personal distress in increasingly medicalized ways.

There are however units throughout the country which seek to avoid such pitfalls and which have developed innovative approaches to marital therapy in clinic settings which are explicitly sceptical of earlier medical and psychiatric orthodoxies. They may include purpose-built residential units (Haldane, McCluskey and Peacey 1980) and those organized on therapeutic community lines (Morrice 1981). To undertake marital or any other form of therapy in these settings is to constantly confront issues in the definition of 'health' and 'sickness'. Staff will find it far less easy to label and diagnose patients in ways which imply personal pathology or dysfunction and will discover the need to develop a more open, sharing style of decision-making, both with patients and with colleagues.

We are aware of interesting innovations, experiments and creative attempts to develop marital work in a variety of primary care settings (Blum 1983; Cohen and Halpern 1978; Toynbee 1983; Watkins 1983). Most of these revolve around attempts to deploy 'practice counsellors' who undertake work with patients on a variety of problems relating to personal life. Counsellors working in this way appear to be growing in number, and examples can probably be found in most parts of the country; but they rest in all cases upon the determination of individual practitioners to develop and maintain such a service. They exist in spite of rather than because of any policy on the part of government departments or health authorities actively to promote such work. Huge opportunities exist to develop marital work in general practice, as well as in health visiting, in psychiatry, in genito-urinary medicine, in the psychological services and increasingly, in the context of multidisciplinary community care. We find it highly unlikely however that any of these will be developed in the near future, other than in a piecemeal and arbitrary manner.

OTHER DOORS

Although we have concentrated here, in this rather superficial review, on the main specialist agencies and the major outlets for marital work in the statutory services, this is not to imply that advice-giving, counselling and therapy are unavailable in other organizations, within the statutory, private or voluntary sectors. From time to time some form of marital work may be conducted in departments of obstetrics and gynaecology; in mother and baby, 'well woman' or family-planning clinics; in drop-in or day centres run by local authorities; in family centres or residential homes of various kinds (we are aware for example of a growing interest in working with marital problems on the part of the wardens of old peoples' homes). Citizens' Advice Bureaux, whose services have been in increasing demand in recent years, report cases involving special marital problems at levels more than double those seen by the specialist marital agencies. The bureaux have the advantages of being widely available on high streets, accessible and sufficiently generic in the services offered to reduce clients' anxieties about entering and seeking help. As with the statutory social services however, they also report a growing need to concentrate their work on issues of welfare rights, not least in a period of major change in the system of social security payments. We doubt therefore whether the bureaux are in a position to develop services in marital work, though they may well be able to engage in more fruitful collaborations with the marriage guidance councils, such as sharing of premises, mutual referral and joint training.

Some readers may be surprised that we have so far said nothing about help for marital problems which may be available from the churches. For even in a society which has been subjected to massive processes of secularization, there remains a sense in which for some people, perhaps along with the family doctor, the clergyman, priest or minister is still regarded as the most obvious person to turn to in times of personal difficulty. Since a significant proportion of marriages continue to be formalized in the church, we might assume that couples who subsequently experience difficulties would, given the churches' wider pastoral role, consider returning there for some form of help. We know that the issue of pastoral care for couples with marital problems has exercised a good deal of debate within the churches. Much of this indeed has been very close to home, in the recognition that clergy and ministers may themselves encounter difficulties in their marriages, which flow in part from the particular features of their occupation. So discussion is taking place about these issues, and help is being provided in a variety of ways. In particular there have been efforts to raise the profile of marriage and family problems within the training of ministers and priests; there has been explicit attention given to the development of counselling skills, and a variety of psychodynamic and group experiences have been incorporated into pastoral training. These are welcome developments, but they do not imply that all newly trained ministers of religion will be equipped to carry out marital work, though a proportion would almost certainly see this as part of their activities.

THE CONCILIATION SERVICES

Finally, we turn to an area which has undergone major developments in recent years, and which though not central to the conception of marital work that we are seeking to formulate here, is nevertheless sufficiently close to merit attention. The argument for a specialized conciliation service for couples in the process of separation and divorce was intially developed by the Finer Committee, which published its report in 1974. The Bristol Courts Family Conciliation Service, established in 1978, was the first attempt to develop a systematic service of this kind in Britain and since then conciliation services have mushroomed throughout the country. Parkinson (1986) gives a detailed account of their development in England and Wales. In both Scotland and England, and unlike marriage guidance, the conciliation services have been subject to government-sponsored evaluation (Matheson and Gentleman 1986; Report of the Conciliation Project Unit 1989).

Although it is our impression that counsellors, therapists and others involved in various ways with marital work are now quite familiar with the concept of conciliation in relation to divorce procedures, it is probably the case that others are confused, not least potential clients. Most of this confusion centres around the distinction between *reconciliation* and *conciliation*. We believe it is prudent to regard both of these as processes, rather than outcomes; they signify in each case movements towards a particular state, the exploration of the meaning of that state and perhaps agreement about how it might be constituted. In neither case do we see the possibility of clearly recognizable, quantifiable or measurable outcomes, though these are certainly being looked for in the case of concilation. By *reconciliation* then we would understand a process which seeks to overcome, reformulate and ameliorate difficulties in the marriage relationship, usually though not always, in the context of the marriage remaining intact as a legal entity. *Conciliation*, however, begins from the assumption that the marriage, as a legal entity, will end or has ended; the task is then to reduce levels of personal distress for those involved, and to make appropriate agreements about the personal and material consequences. The definition used by Finer still appears to be in working use by others and gives comprehensive coverage of the conciliation process: 'assisting the parties to deal with the consequences of the established breakdown of their marriage . . . by reaching agreements or giving consents or reducing the area of conflict upon custody, support, access to and education of the children, financial provision, the disposition of the marital home, laywers' fees, and every other matter arising from the breakdown which calls for a decision on future arrangements' (DHSS 1974:176).

This definition of course raises numerous questions about how such a service should be organized and the skills which would be required of the conciliators. This latter question has been discussed in some detail by James and Wilson (1986) and we do not wish to develop the argument here, except to note that conciliation's emphasis upon a more task-focused, contractual and time-limited style of working and its recognition and willingness to engage with the complex interactions between the public and private elements of marriage and divorce, has much in common with the model of consultation to which we have already referred in detail in part 3.

It is relevant however, given our concern with organizational issues, to say something about the ways in which conciliation services are developing and the relationship which they might have with other marital agencies. It is clear from a reading of the marriage guidance literature and from observing the scene in general, that there has been some ambivalence on the part of the marriage guidance councils about how conciliation services might be organized. Tyndall, a former chief officer of the NMGC, makes this clear, for example, in stating that 'conciliators require sufficient experience of marital work to give them a confident understanding of interaction between couples,' a clear reference to the suitability of marriage guidance counsellors, given further training, for this work. But he also cautions against unrealistic expectations of conciliation and asks rather sceptically, 'If the needs for this service are now so obvious to everyone, why has it taken nearly 20 years of rising divorce figures for us to recognise this?' (1982:116, 117). This ambivalence is reflected in the overall pattern of development of conciliation services and the involvement of marriage guidance personnel. Representatives of the latter have been active on steering groups and management committees of conciliation services throughout the country; and a number of marriage guidance counsellors have become conciliators. But the conciliation service has in no sense become an extension of the work of the marriage guidance councils. This is perhaps surprising given the existence of an infrastructure of buildings, personnel and procedures for selecting, training and supervising workers. There are of course many reasons why the instigators of a new service would not wish to hitch themselves irrevocably to an existing one, especially given the problems which the marriage guidance councils have faced. But it does seem to us regrettable that given the imagination and talent for innovation that undoubtedly exists, some more determined effort could not have been made to forge the basis for a more integrated 'single door' service.

Instead, and in the absence of any promise of central government funding for conciliation, at least until such time as the results of a major research project funded by the Lord Chancellor's Office have been received, local developments in conciliation in England and Wales take place on a gradualist and fragmented basis, within the context of a mixed economy of funding. Some local services run on shoestring budgets almost entirely as a result of voluntary endeavour. Others receive local authority support, employ coordinators and are able to pay their conciliators on a sessional basis. The position in Scotland is slightly different; here Scottish Office funding has been made available to support the formation of the Scottish Association of Family Conciliation Services, and, helped by the smaller number of local initiatives, it has been possible to develop a nationally coordinated approach to service development. Throughout Britain however, the future for concilation services is unclear and it seems likely that for the forseeable time technical issues in the development of conciliation as a form of intervention will go hand in hand with financial and other anxieties which affect the possibilities for service provision.

In England and Wales this leaves the divorce court welfare officers in a particularly important role. Their work has recently been looked at in detail in a study by Clulow and Vincent (1987). The authors describe the divorce process as 'the meshing of private complaint and public response' (1987:3), in which court welfare officers not only provide personal support to divorcing couples and seek private settlements between them, but at the same time investigate the circumstances of the couples' lives, particularly in relation to the children. Although the couples seen by these officers are only a small proportion of the divorcing population, Clulow and Vincent show that like that population, they are weighted towards the lower end of the social class register. There is also some evidence that they may be overrepresentative of cases in which the 'behaviour' clause is used to establish the grounds for divorce. These are cases characterized by particularly high levels of conflict and contest in which spouses found 'irresistible' the tendency to attribute to others 'all that was blameworthy and reprehensible' (Clulow and Vincent 1987:209). It seems likely that an adversarial legal system is particularly well matched to the emotional needs of such spouses around the period of divorce. We have commented at various points that the notion of the 'civilized', 'no fault' divorce is usually experienced as more apparent than real. There is now an overwhelming case for effective concilia-tion services to be developed and made widely available, both in and out of the courts.

CROSSING THE THRESHOLD

Whichever of these distinct agency doors is approached, in order to cross the threshold it will be necessary for the client couple to articulate an acceptable reason for entry. This need not always require that some account of the problem is necessarily given to the 'gatekeeper', usually a receptionist; in marriage guidance councils for instance it is normally sufficient simply to request an appointment. Nevertheless it is likely that the couple, and particularly the wife, have given some attention to the expression of the 'problem', a kind of socially validated reason for entry, if acknowledged only to themselves. As we have implied already, this will be a process shaped by a variety of personal, cultural, ideological and material factors. The 'ticket of entry' may state a problem of personal health, concern about the behaviour of another, such as a spouse or child, a social or economic problem or one requiring legal advice. In some cases wife or couple may feel compelled to cast this in 'crisis' terms, as a way of achieving entry or at least of legitimizing their request. This may secure an early appointment in some social work or medical settings. It is less likely to attract special or expeditious attention in the marriage guidance service. Within that system, at least in some areas, there has been a resistance to so-called 'crisis intervention', the preference being to respond by offering an appointment, even though this may be many weeks ahead. There seems to be a view, if not a formulated policy, that a waiting period prior to the first session has a certain therapeutic value of its own, as if this offered the waiting spouse or couple the opportunity to prepare for the 'first interview'. Whatever the assumption or expectation, it is clearly also the period during which the spouse or couple decide not to keep the first appointment, a situation not unfamiliar in the secondary care system of the National Health Service, that is, in hospitals.

From studies such as those of Brannen and Collard (1982) and of Hunt (1985) we know that wives tend to hope for help that will be emotionally supportive; a substitute perhaps for that which is lacking in their experience of their husbands. Husbands, for their part, look for advice and programmes of action, perhaps in a continued search for change which they can control. As Haldane (1988) has shown, it may be difficult, for a number of reasons, for spouse or couple to get what they want or what they feel they need. Firstly, they may not be clear about what they want or need and have only a partial impression or no idea at all of what is on offer; we have been dismayed on a number of occasions to hear this described as the clients 'inappropriate expectations' of the agency. Secondly, to articulate a request may be difficult enough and to negotiate a response may be even more so, especially in the role of supplicant; this says a great deal about the relative power differential which may even from the outset have placed its stamp on the 'therapeutic relationship'. Thirdly, most couples are unlikely to be at all versed in the rules and procedures which determine the responses of potential therapists; nor are they likely to be aware that the person they first see may need to reformulate their problem in order to match it with the organizational responses available. Finally, the response may be significantly determined by factors and policies which are unlikely to be explicitly discussed with those who seek help. These organizational constraints will be familiar to workers in the field of marital counselling and therapy. They often find expression in statements such as 'at present we take all comers, believing that our form of help is potentially beneficial for everyone, if only they will conform to a certain approach'; or 'during training our workers are introduced to our ideology – the belief that clients can benefit from a caring relationship in which to explore the nature of their difficulties'; or 'it is inappropriate for clients to come expecting advice or information when it is therapy, or counselling, or casework that is on offer.' So also in a number of settings a major aim of the first meeting may be, in the unfortunate phrase so often found in professional articles, to 'weed out' those who are considered 'unsuitable for treatment'. Even when there is an agreement to offer some form of counselling or therapy there may remain further uncertainties. The person who makes the offer may be conducting a reception or intake interview, so someone else may do the therapy. The assessor may be a senior practitioner who may delegate the therapy to a junior colleague for experience. Or the assessor and potential therapist may be the most junior, least experienced member of a team, for example the basic grade social worker whose task is to implement the statutory responsibilities of the social services – a long list which does not include marital therapy. In some cases whoever takes on the therapy may not have access to either consultation or supervision. Certainly the level and nature of training that person has received will be highly variable both within and between agencies (Haldane 1988).

TRAINING FOR MARITAL WORK

Many of the staff undertaking marital work in the statutory and voluntary agencies had hoped that the 1980s would be a period of expansion of better organized and more appropriate training. *Marriage Matters* had indicated how limited was the available training both for those who came across marital problems only in the course of other work and for the voluntary agencies engaged specifically in marital work. It was also noted that there were only the most minimal resources for the training of those who sought to become specialist practitioners and trainers. The report therefore proposed the establishment of 'marital training and development groups', to be locally organized but centrally funded. None of these recommendations has yet been implemented. In Scotland, interviewing and sending questionnaires to a cohort of psychiatrists, clinical psychologists and social workers known to be working with couples, Haldane and McCluskey's findings (1980; 1981) supported those of the report and indicated how much had to be developed before achieving the standards defined by Kaslow (1977) for American practice.

These reports show that in the primary training of doctors, social workers, psychologists, nurses, or other practitioners in the statutory services, no priority is given to the study of marriage and its problems: indeed, such study occupies a minimal place in the programme of training, if at all. Nor does it feature to any significant degree in post-qualification training. There is no evidence of any major development of resources devoted to training in these professions and the relative brevity of the chapters on training in Dryden's (1985) two-volume review of *Marital Therapy in Britain* confirms this. That there is a gradual increase in the availability of courses of training is shown by the advertisements in the *Newsletter* of the Association for Family Therapy, but such courses are offered in a very few places and in some the focus on marital work is secondary to a training in family therapy. It is difficult to know whether the lack of *research* into training is a cause or consequence of these deficiencies. but they are as evident now (Haldane 1988) as they were almost a decade earlier (Walrond-Skinner 1979).

For those in professional practice who want to develop some training in marital work, the most readily available possibilities, providing they are selected, are the courses offered by the marriage guidance councils. They can then put this training to use, not only on a part time, voluntary basis, but within their own organizational settings. In our view the absence of opportunities to develop further expertise in marital work stands in sharp contrast to the kinds of post-basic facilities which may exist for further training in such cognate areas as general counselling skills, issues in child abuse, HIV infection and AIDS or work on aspects of sexuality.

This not only further underlines the low priority which marital work has in the statutory agencies, with all the attendant questions, to which we shall later turn, of why this should be the case; it also raises questions about whether the skills, methodology and philosophy of 'marriage guidance' can appropriately be transferred to the organizational, political and professional structures of these statutory services. This question, as far as we are aware, has not been evaluated. There is however some evidence that the work of marriage guidance trained counsellors is valued within the statutory agencies. For example there has been a considerable expansion, as we have already noted, in the numbers of counsellors working in general practice settings. Likewise, and dependent to a significant degree on local conditions, personalities and relationships, there are in some localities close working links between voluntary marriage guidance counsellors and the staff of other agencies, with a readiness to refer clients or patients for opinion or further action. We are also aware however that some marriage guidance counsellors have difficulty in asking for a second opinion or asking a professional colleague to 'take on the case', on the grounds that confidentiality of information is paramount. It seems difficult for such counsellors to ask their clients' permission to share information with a colleague from whom help is being sought.

Once again we are reminded of the need to ground issues in the development of marital work in an organizational context. Indeed it may be unwise to talk at all of 'marital work' in isolation from the organizational settings in which it takes place. With this in mind however, we believe there are a number of fundamental questions in relation to training which have been insufficiently addressed. We list some of these here.

If there were more systematic agreement about the aims and objectives of work with couples, there might more readily be agreement about the form and content of training. Much training still concentrates on experiential learning and the potential for 'personal growth' of the trainee counsellor, often at the expense of learning about the dynamics of couple relationships or about the private and public aspects of marriage. Or there may be a slavish adherence to training in skills and to those given prominence by a particular conceptual framework or approach to practice. The debate continues about the proportion of training time which should be devoted to elements of systematic teaching, experiential learning and skills training. While it might seem obvious that some combination of all such approaches is valid, desirable, even necessary, there are some who would give unequivocal emphasis to one, rejecting the others as less important, irrelevant or even potentially damaging to 'proper' training.

If we accept the notion of a more inclusive approach to training in marital work (i.e. one which actively engages with the public and private aspects of the marriage phenomenon), it is still necessary to define the kinds of skills which will be required to conduct therapy or counselling. The definition of these skills, and still more so the clarification of the aims and methods which will be required to train workers in them, is a major undertaking. The more clear we are about the skills which are required and the forms and methods of training necessary to develop them, the more possible it will become to devise appropriate methods of selection for this work. At the moment the most thoroughgoing system of selection (as with many other dimensions of the field) lies with the marriage guidance councils; but even here we are doubtful of the extent to which systematic developments in training have been matched by similar attempts to upgrade selection procedures. World War II officer selection procedures have much that is of value: whether they are the best way of selecting marriage guidance counsellors needs reviewing. Elsewhere, indeed particularly for marital work conducted in social work and clinical settings, selection procedures are distinguished mainly by their absence.

As we shall see in a later section, there is little research evidence to support the greater effectiveness of one model of marital therapy or counselling over another. So no one is in a position to say (though some certainly try) that one particular approach should be the basis of training; once again organizational policies, traditions, inertia, territoriality and sheer stubbornness at times, are often very powerful determinants of a particular agency's 'model' of practice or training. Whether training should be based on one model or conceptual framework, or whether trainees should be exposed to a range of models and their practice consequences, is a debate not peculiar to this kind of training and already familiar in the context of training for psychotherapy or family therapy. It is difficult to assess what is currently on offer, not only whether one or several models is preferred, but also the extent to which practice is seen to be based on any particular model for marital work.

How this question is resolved will, among other consequences, affect the different levels or stages in what ought to be a continuing process of long-term learning and maintaining competence. Given our view that knowledge and skills and competence should be aspects of an integrated process of development over time and as experience is gained, it is necessary to consider the stage of training which is appropriate to 'the beginner' and the ways in which training may be advanced or modified for those who come into this work well prepared by other relevant experience. If we are to think about stages of training such as basic, intermediate and advanced, we must be clear about the differences in aims, methods and the expectations of trainees. Are the later stages of training to focus on acquiring more knowledge about a particular model, or knowledge of other, less familiar models? Ought they to concentrate on the refining and extension of skills or on an extension into new areas of work? Or, indeed, all of these. We are much in need of an informed debate on these matters.

Opinion will also differ about the point at which and under what circumstances the trainee will begin work with couples. How best to monitor the work of trainees with couples is certainly for many a debateable and contentious issue. Not all practitioners, even at the level of trainee or beginner, will consider it appropriate that their work should be monitored and evaluated, far less agree on how and by whom this should be done. These differences and uncertainties are also shared by their trainers. Given these difficulties, it will be apparent that opinions vary about the duration of training, when and by what process the trainee should be assessed and how best the practitioner is to maintain competence. Finally, there is not as yet any national level of agreement about procedures for registration or accreditation in marital work, or about codes of practice. But the discussions necessary to such results have become productive among the many and varied groups practising some form of psychotherapy, so that such definitions of standards might not be long delayed.

At this point it is worth pausing for a moment to consider why all this should be so. In part 2 of this book we have marshalled a variety of evidence which points *in extenso* to the many ways in which marriage in our society, in its various guises and at differing stages of the life course, has become a public issue of major significance. We have also seen, in part 3, that the ideas and range of models which have been developed to offer help to those in marital distress do not lack sophistication. And yet the procedures and systems for training counsellors and therapists in marital work, with the exception, we acknowledge, of the marriage guidance councils, remain limited in availability. There are clearly some political and policy reasons why this should be the case, which themselves reflect on the poorly developed range of services; we shall turn to these towards the end of this section. For the moment it is worth exploring in a little detail some of the more fundamental reasons why marital work of various kinds and the training which is required in order to undertake it, appear so underdeveloped, fragmentary, hidden and poorly esteemed within the helping professions.

PROBLEMS OF MARITAL WORK

We believe that one explanation for all this rests with some of the intrinsic qualities and contradictions of marital work; in particular, the ways in which such work takes place on the boundary between the private and public domains. We referred earlier to the reflection processes and dynamics which can occur within the organizational context of marital work and in the working relationship between couple and consultant. Experience of supervision clearly indicates, not unexpectedly, that practitioners are influenced in their work by their own marriages and those of their parents. Not all of those who undertake marital work are married themselves and some limited evidence suggests that recent cohorts of trainee marriage guidance counsellors are significantly overrepresented in the proportions that are divorced and/or remarried (Semeonoff 1985). There seems to be no particular reason why practitioners in their personal lives should be any less likely to encounter the wider social context of marital problems, of separation and of divorce. A major question, about which we have little evidence, is the extent to which the personal experience of marriage of the practitioner, especially at the trainee stage, is and should be taken into account as a major factor affecting attitudes and competence.

Aspects of congruence and dissonance between the personal experience of therapist and client have been particularly addressed by feminist psychotherapists, who have developed a strong commitment to engaging with those aspects of gendered experience which women may share and which will have touched the lives of both 'therapist' and 'client' (Greenspan 1983). In doing this, therapists such as Greenspan and Eichenbaum and Orbach(1984) have also been prepared to explore their work in its public context, of a society which systematically determines a variety of personal experiences and public opportunities on the basis of gender. This is relevant to marital work in two important ways. First, any reading of key works in the field of marital therapy will reveal an unreconstructed approach to issues of sex and gender. For whatever reasons, feminist thinking and practice have been slow to take a hold in marital work, a point illustrated by Morgan (1985) when reviewing the recommended reading for trainee marriage guidance counsellors and certainly echoed in our own experience of direct work with the marital agencies. Second, it is highly relevant to the views and expectations which individual therapists may have of marriage as an institution which, in a variety of ways – differences in health, earning capacity, employment opportunities, the division of unpaid domestic labour – significantly discriminates against the interests of women. How far can and should such issues be relevant to working with couples? Counselling orthodoxies of the recent past, with their emphasis on self-empowerment, choice and personal growth, suggest an ethical neutrality on this issue which appears to us more and more difficult to maintain in the light of available evidence and a rapidly changing discourse of marriage in society.

It can be argued of course that this neutrality was itself socially constructed and reflected those changes, referred to earlier in relation to the marriage guidance councils, which sought to represent the move from 'advice' to 'counselling': in other words a shift from the purposive guidance of marriage 'experts' to the therapautic relationship provided by the trained counsellor. The implication of this is that there are no paradigms for a 'good' marriage, still less for one which is morally 'correct' or 'Christian'. These now rather self-evident views are of course historically very recent ones; it is useful to remind ourselves that they have pervaded our culture only over the last few decades. They clearly have implications for the attitudes of those who work with couples. They may not however fully accord with the expectations that couples have of therapy, counselling or the agencies that provide them.

Another way of formulating some of this is by considering the problems which must be resolved in order for marital counselling or therapy to take place effectively. These concern the interrelationships between factors which are personal, or professional, or organizational. We have noted in relation to psychotherapy training (Haldane, Alexander and Walker 1982), that it would be unrealistic to assume that those who undertake training in marital work could always lay claim to a mature level of integration in their personality development, however that might be defined. Adequate training recognizes such limitations, not necessarily so that 'treatment' may be offered, but so that trainees can appreciate the ways in which these factors may limit their own effectiveness as therapists, and take action to minimize them. It is safe to assume that marital therapists, like others, enter their work for a variety of motives and with a range of needs, which however unconsciously, they seek to satisfy. It would be quite wrong to pretend that these motives are all positive or that the needs are commonplace; they must therefore be identified and worked through in training. Linked to this is the question of the trainee therapist's capacity to acknowledge, cope with, perhaps accept, frustration and failure, both in his or her own work and in the lives of the clients. This makes the continuing use of systems of personal and professional support an essential prerequisite of effective marital work – a point which also holds for counselling and psychotherapy more generally.

There is now a growing corpus of knowledge about marital work, much of it highly relevant to the effective working of both trainee and more experienced therapists alike. It remains however a disparate body of material and one which requires diligence and tenacity to uncover. Its fragmentary nature reflects the varied and partial organizational context in which marital work is currently taking place and the often very limited overlap or exchange between the different services and agencies involved. It is revealed also in the limited opportunities which exist for marital work as a full-time occupation or profession and the lack of any form of career structure. Social workers, psychiatrists, psychologists, nurses and others working in the statutory health and social services may have little time or opportunity for this work or may even be actively discouraged from undertaking it. Conversely, some volunteers in the marriage guidance services may, on the basis of that experience, seek professional training and employment in one of the statutory caring agencies, only to find that there are few if any possibilities for undertaking the kind of work which had first inspired and motivated them. This can be exacerbated by interprofessional rivalries and differences about who rightfully 'owns' marital work and who is most competent to conduct it. It is hardly surprising therefore that the one growth area for marital counselling and therapy is in the fee-paying sector of private practice, where individual workers may develop their interests and skills relatively free from professional and organizational constraints, but perhaps also without either supervision or support.

Practitioners therefore require both the authority and the permission or freedom to carry out marital work. For those who work privately, authority stems from a self-assessment of competence and the willingness of clients to come directly or by referral to pay for the services which they offer. By contrast, for those who work in a statutory service or voluntary organization, authority, accountability and responsibility will take a variety of forms which must be familiar to and understood by the individual practitioner. As we have seen, in some caring organizations it cannot be assumed that the practice of marital work will be uncritically supported; in certain settings it may even be sabotaged, however covertly, in favour of other forms of intervention or service delivery. Whether taken individually or in some combination, it is clear that a variety of constraints, limitations and pitfalls is likely to beset anyone with an interest in and desire to develop marital work as part of their practice. We do not pretend that these factors are absent from other forms of counselling and psychotherapy; we do believe however that they can be particularly exacerbated in marital work, making it a field of intervention which is particularly difficult both to enter and remain in to any good effect.

LIMITATIONS ON SERVICE DEVELOPMENT

It should by now be clear that we regard as inadequate the present level of services available to couples seeking help in their relationships. But it is not difficult to see why this is the case. Even the high levels of divorce and remarriage which we have shown to be persistent features of our culture, and which are generally acknowledged to be problematic in a variety of ways, do not automatically produce particular organizational responses. For one thing, there are competing demands on the budgets available to health and social services; and there are plenty of other, perhaps outwardly more pressing claims for support. We have noted how linked social problems, such as child or alcohol abuse, seem consistently to exercise the minds of policy-makers and the general public, in ways which marital problems do not. It seems to us that the limited development of services for couples is underpinned by the view that relationship difficulties do not belong in the public arena and should not be 'owned' by statutory agencies, though voluntary organizations may wish to be involved, providing they are not too much of a drain on the public purse. According to this rhetoric, problems in relationships are the private business of those involved and should remain their responsibility; couples make their own beds and should be left to lie on them. This is of course a partial view, and there is no shortage of the opposite argument which says that personal distress, if it is to be effectively resolved, requires the help of skilled professionals. But it remains the case that skilled help in relation to marital relationships is not widely and easily available; at best it is seen by policy-makers as a desirable but presently unaffordable service, at worst as an irrelevance of unrestrained and haphazard meddling in the private world of family life.

Such are the contradictions of *wedlock*, of relationship and institution, of personal freedom and social constraint; it is hardly surprising that ambivalence, even denial, characterize attitudes to services for couples. We are aware from our own experience of the marriage guidance councils, at both local and national level, that government agencies tend to marginalize marital problems, deeming them to be either not on the agenda of public responsibility or too complex and intractable to merit intervention. They are seen as either beyond the day-to-day responsibilities of the 'caring professions', or as requiring extensive and unaffordable further training for the relevant workers. It is also a fact, much emphasized by funding agencies, that such services are difficult to evaluate and do not comfortably fit with the call for 'performance indicators'.

One concern about the services provided is that they may be restricted in the range of clients they serve. In particular, there may be imbalances relating to social class. A common conception among workers in the field, for example, is that middle-class couples are most likely to find their way to the marriage guidance councils, whereas working-class couples, if they are able to find any help at all, are most likely to be seen by workers in the statutory social services. This is a perception which is still to be tested out by careful research, and which has so far not been answered by the internal monitoring of the marital agencies themselves. In seeking to answer this question it is worth keeping in mind that, as we have already seen, divorce takes place at a disproportionately high rate among social classes IV and V. It is doubtful whether this issue of social class has been sufficiently addressed within the marital agencies, though it may have very real implications for the modes of intervention which are on offer. It is likely that the subjective experience of marital problems will vary according to social class, shaping the ways in which men and women respond and setting limits on the most effective forms of help.

Perhaps most of all, what limits the development of services for those distressed in their marital relationships is not funding, or organization, or personnel, or training, or other limitations on best practice, but acknowledged difficulties in doing such work. No one who works with couples can themselves be devoid of experiences, attitudes, feelings about marriage. Marriage and its problems are for most of us matters which are well known and deeply felt. A recurring experience in discussions with practitioners is that marital work offers particular difficulties, not encountered by those whose main work is with individuals, or with families, or with groups. Whatever the explanation of these difficulties, it is best that they are not denied.

4.2 Problems of Research

In exploring the organizational contexts where help is offered to couples in their relationships we have been at pains to point out the dynamics and structures which can influence development, positively or negatively. In moving now to the question of research into marriage and marital work, we shall try to maintain the same focus, paying attention to the settings in which such work takes place. We shall see that the kind of work which is being carried out is again linked to political and policy agendas of various kinds and that there are some major divisions in approach which are in part a product of professional and disciplinary boundaries. For heuristic purposes however we shall make the distinction between *formal* and *applied* areas of work. We are not implying by this that some researchers are exclusively interested in formal research, academically orientated to the theoretical and methodological concerns of their particular discipline. Or indeed that others are focused only on questions of practitioner relevance, and to that extent are largely unconcerned with issues of theory and method. But there are two discernible lines of development which have been pursued fairly independently; and part of our task will be to explore how these might be more effectively integrated.

When we refer to the *formal* tradition of marriage research we think less of particular disciplinary studies than of ways of asking questions. Research in this tradition is about asking *how* questions. *How* is the institution of marriage in our society shaped by variables like social class, patterns of employment, mobility or life expectancy? *How* have the meanings, both public and personal, which surround marriage been changing over time? *How* are individual marriages constituted, dissolved and reconstituted through the life course? This kind of research is therefore concerned with marriage as a personal and social *phenomenon*; it recognizes that our taken-for-granted understanding of marriage in society must be treated with the utmost caution and that the values, beliefs, assertions and attitudes which attach themselves to marriage are friable and precarious social constructions. This research belongs to a sceptical tradition whose only canon is that, in the social world, things are never what they seem.

Applied research starts from a very different place. This kind of work is less concerned with how a given phenomenon, marriage, is socially constructed than with the implications of certain perceptions of marriage current in society at a particular time. Researchers in this tradition will therefore be much more likely to accept someone else's definition of the situation as their starting point. In this case that could mean for example accepting that marriage in our society has become a 'problem' in certain ways, some of which we have referred to in earlier sections. A good example of this is the assumption that there is a category of phenomena which can be called 'marital problems' and which have been defined by 'experts' of various kinds

– counsellors, therapists, policy-makers, other researchers – so that the task is now to evaluate how best they can be alleviated, through the provision of services offering various forms of intervention. Our researcher will now be asking questions like *why* are services organized in particular ways? *Which* are the most effective types of intervention? And *what* are the criteria for success?

There are various relationships between these two positions. For one thing the former might regard the latter as a research subject in its own right, asking how it is that the apparently private world of relationships can be constructed as a problem and seeking to understand the role which research may have in that process. For example, the part played by researchers in collecting data on the extent of 'marital problems' cannot be separated from the process of defining marriage as a social problem more generally. Or it might be argued that researchers into marital problems form part of a wider social enterprise which is concerned to open up the private worlds of marriage and personal or family relationships and in so doing make them more amenable to control and intervention by state agencies, what Donzelot (1980) has called the *policing* of families.

Alternatively, the researcher who begins with a pre-defined subject, let us say one identified by a marital agency, will soon find that 'the problem' has numerous facets. It may be defined differently by different personnel within the agency; or there may be important mismatches between the way it is perceived by the agency and by its clients. The researcher will then be in the position of having to reformulate the question, perhaps to the extent of turning it into something which is researchable at all, while being guided and perhaps constrained by the organizational context in which the research is to take place.

Let us take an imaginary example of this. A medium-sized marriage guidance council has a problem with its main funding body, the social services committee of the local authority. The committee receives annual reports of the number of clients seen by the council, it is told how many clients come individually or in couples and it is given information about how many times they are seen. However, some committee members are concerned to know more about what goes on with these clients: what is the counselling about, what are the main problems presented and how are they dealt with? A few members ask whether the council is being successful in its 'main aim' of keeping couples out of the divorce courts; some want to know what is being done to safeguard the interests of children whose parents are having marital problems; still others point to the competing claims of other voluntary agencies seeking grant aid for their work with rape victims, gay men and women, wives who have been beaten by their husbands and people with alcohol problems; and ask whether, in comparison, the council is offering value for money? The marriage guidance council decides it needs to get some 'hard' evidence to portray the 'good work' which it is doing; these things can no longer be taken on trust, the council must move with the times and carry out some form of evaluation. The local polytechnic has therefore been approached and, for a fee, has agreed to provide a researcher who will carry out the necessary work.

It would be inaccurate to say that this is where the problems *begin*, since clearly they are already well developed and multifaceted; but at this point a number of complex issues will have to be addressed if any effective research can be carried out. The council may draft a brief for the reseacher to study 'outcomes' among a sample of its clients. This may include research into 'consumer satisfaction' as well as subsequent circumstances in the lives of the couples: do they stay together, separate or divorce? The researcher may, with reservations, accept this and go on to produce an appropriate research design. This would, in essence, be the response of the researcher working in the 'applied' tradition. On the other hand, the researcher may feel uncomfortable in working to a brief prepared by the council, may wish to work more collaboratively and spend some time in discussion with members about the aims and objectives of the research. Again, this may be containable within the circumscribed boundary of a piece of evaluation research. But other researchers may wish to go further: they may want to know more precisely why and on what authority the research is being requested; they may sense anxieties within the agency, conflicting interests, suspicions, the fear of coming 'under the microscope'; they may detect political manoeuvring and the desire to use research findings to 'prove' the case for the agency's continued funding. They may acknowledge that all marital agencies are facing difficulties in developing their work within the context of changing social trends and values and suggest that these wider factors cannot be disentangled from the particular brief which has been prepared.

These are but a few examples of the many problems which may be confronted by social researchers in the field of marital work. They show how the researcher must, while sharpening up the formulation of the research problem at hand, be prepared to engage with a range of factors which take in the wider social context. Research based on clinical models finds this difficult to tolerate, seeking to eliminate or control as far as possible 'environmental' factors which may have

differential effects on outcomes. We believe that these are inappropriate models for evaluation in marital work, other than perhaps where
the therapy in use is unabashedly behavioural, and that we should
seek instead to develop methods of research which are more syntonic
with the range of interventions in use. As we shall see, this argument
also applies to those working on more 'formal' studies of marriage.

Of course, the distinction between formal and applied work is
increasingly a false one. A variety of pressures which now exist in
higher education and social research have forced researchers to be
more consumer- and market-led in the construction of research
problems. This can have welcome results, but it can also be unhelpful,
for example when the market becomes the sole determinant of the
problem or when its needs always predominate over those for more
fundamental inquiry. As we have seen, *Marriage Matters* advocated
the formation of multidisciplinary units in which research and
intervention in marriage might be pursued in a collaborative manner.
Only two centres, the Tavistock Institute of Marital Studies and the
Marriage Research Centre have developed this pattern to any significant degree, and both of these predate the Home Office report.

The Tavistock Institute of Marital Studies (TIMS) was established in
1948 and for its first 20 years was known as the Family Discussion
Bureau; originally under the auspicies of the Family Welfare Association, it transferred to the Tavistock Institute of Human Relations in
the mid-1950s, and later to the Tavistock Institute of Medical Psychology, where it has since remained. TIMS staff are practising marital
therapists, who also provide training and consultation to workers in a
range of other agencies and conduct research. These combined skills
have resulted in a number of major studies. We have already referred
on several occasions to Mattinson and Sinclair's (1979) classic account
of marital work in a local authority social work department. Clulow
(1980) has also reported an interesting piece of action research in
which TIMS staff took part with a group of London health visitors in
developing a support network for couples coping with the arrival of a
first baby. This was followed by a fascinatingly detailed portrayal of
marital therapy with a single couple (Clulow 1986) and more recently
by studies of the work of divorce court welfare officers (Clulow and
Vincent 1987) and of the effects of unemployment on marriage
(Mattinson 1988). Workers at the TIMS operate from a psychodynamic perspective which places a particular emphasis upon the ways in
which problematic relationships in adulthood may be determined by
experiences in earlier life of close, two-person relationships. As we
shall see later, this provides a level of understanding which is

significantly missing from most recent studies of marriage, the majority of which are written from a sociological rather than a psychological perspective.

A number of sociological studies of marriage and its problems have been produced by the Marriage Research Centre at the Central Middlesex Hospital. The Marriage Research Centre was founded in 1971 with two principal aims: 'on the one hand to undertake research relating to contemporary marriage and, on the other, to provide a clinical service for marital therapy and courses for practitioners with an interest in marital work' (Brannen and Collard 1982:xii). Apart from a range of general publications by its director, which focus mainly on clinical issues in marital work (Dominian 1969; 1979), the centre has produced three important empirical studies. Thornes and Collard (1979) produced a social demographic study of a sample of the divorcing population. Brannen and Collard (1982), whose work we have referred to on a number of occasions, carried out an important investigation into help-seeking among a group of couples who sought therapy and counselling; these writers were among the first in Britain to begin to explore the helping process from a sociological perspective. Finally, the centre has conducted a longitudinal study of a group of couples who married for the first time in 1979 and who were interviewed shortly afterwards, and again five years later (Mansfield and Collard 1988).

With the exception of these two small units, we are unable to cite any other centres currently seeking to develop a range of activities which combines research, training and practice in marital work. It is true that during the mid-1980s the National Marriage Guidance Council conducted and published the results of a number of research studies, all of them relating to concerns within the agency, but it is not clear whether research will remain a significant priority on the agenda of the reconstituted organization, Relate. The other marriage guidance councils have so far not developed a sustained approach to research. So the marital agencies are not in general to be seen as centres for research into marriage, still less at the forefront of new substantive, theoretical or methodological innovation. How far this is a product simply of inadequate resources, or of some more fundamental reasons for not becoming involved, is difficult to determine. We do note once again, however, that like other agencies within the caring services, these tend to regard research as a relatively low priority, something which at best confirms what practitioners already know and at worst gets in the way of the primary task of helping those in distress.

Fortunately however, it is possible to identify some areas of growth and development in marriage research in recent years, although these have been somewhat piecemeal and haphazard. For a variety of reasons the late 1970s saw an upturn in the numbers of professional academics and postgraduate students interested in conducting research into aspects of marriage and family life. Indeed, having for a long period been a somewhat Cinderella area of the social sciences, study in this field has now gained a certain popularity. This has in large measure been due to the widespread influence of feminism, and particularly the encouragement which women's studies have given to research into aspects of domestic life. Those aspects of the social world which have traditionally in our society been the preserve of women: domestic labour, child care, caring for elderly relations, have been released from the accumulated assumptions which assigned them to the backwaters of intellectual inquiry. Feminist debate in the 1970s not only made the personal political, but also encouraged serious discussion and inquiry on issues about relationships and resources within households and families.

There are a number of individuals in polytechnics, colleges, universities and units throughout the country who are currently involved in research and teaching around marriage, family and domestic issues. It is true that this work tends to be less concerned with issues about couples and partnerships than with the structural arrangements which surround the institution of marriage and interconnect it with other areas, such as patterns of child care, women's employment or informal care of dependent relatives. But an important effect of this interest has been to bring together researchers and practitioners in mutual exchange and discussion. We detect a welcome shift here in the willingness of social researchers to become actively involved in questions about policy and service development. Some of this can be traced in the following sections where we explore in more detail the growth in marriage research and service evaluation in recent decades.

RESEARCHING MARRIAGES

Although most commentators on the changes which have taken place in British family and domestic life since World War II emphasize the importance of marriage as a now almost universal experience, there is far less agreement about the direction and significance of change within marriage itself. There are a number of reasons for this. Beliefs safeguarding the privacy of domestic life in general and couple relationships in particular, make it very difficult to know what goes on in families and households from day to day. This is often compounded by an uncritical acceptance of social arrangements surrounding the family as something determined by the facts of human nature and therefore requiring no explanation or interpretation (La Fontaine 1985). Paradoxically, changes in patterns of marriage and divorce over the period, which have to some extent undermined the 'naturalness' of these arrangements, have als turned marriage and partnership into a *public issue*, which as Wright Mills (1959) points out, has the potential to threaten 'cherished values'. In this sense marriage and family life become objects of concern and speculation on the part of a wide range of social commentators, researchers, policy-makers and practitioners. Anyone who reads newspapers and magazines, listens to the radio or watches television will know that marriage is a popular subject for discussion. They will also recognize that it is a subject ridden with contradictions.

Many different kinds of evidence are used to support the view that changes in patterns of postwar domestic life have generated *qualitatively* different expectations and experiences of marriage. This evidence has often been gathered for a variety of differing purposes, and so presents problems of comparison. But sociologists and demographers agree that over 90 per cent of the population will be legally married at least once in their lives (Rimmer 1981); and despite a significant increase in divorce and remarriage, it is calculated that on present trends between two-thirds and three-quarters of today's newly-weds will remain married to one another until the death of one or other partner (Haskey 1982). Likewise, the proportion of married couples who become parents has risen in the postwar years, though completed family size has become smaller (Rimmer 1981).

These trends were linked in the 1950s and 1960s to an increase in the available housing stock, both public and private, and were accompanied by the growing expectation that newly married couples would have 'a place of their own' in which to 'start a family'. Such phrases illustrate tacit and taken-for-granted beliefs about the norms of domestic arrangements: marriage, followed by child-bearing and the nuclear family unit independently housed. In the wake of this came a major debate which revolved around the extent to which the 'extended' family had gone into terminal decline.

Research conducted by sociologists and social psychologists at the Institute of Community Studies played a central part in this controversy. In particular the 'Bethnal Green trilogy' (Young and Willmot 1957; Townsend 1957; and Marris 1958) explored various aspects of family life in that part of London: kinship relations, the lives of old people and widowhood. These studies showed in fine detail how patterns of domestic life, and in particular the relationships between spouses, could be affected by external factors, such as slum clearance policies and the creation of suburban housing estates. They documented a shift from marriage and family life as part of a wider network of kinship and community ties to a situation in which couples and families led a socially more isolated existence, where domestic life was increasingly valued for its own intrinsic rewards.

Published around the same time, Elizabeth Bott's *Family and Social Network* (1957), a study which had been carried out from the Tavistock Institute, cast further light on these processes, with particular reference to the conjugal relationship. Bott sought to explain contrasting styles of marriage by reference to the sorts of social network which couples inhabit. Her work, which still has a great deal of relevance today, showed how couples with a relatively *separated* conjugal relationship, in which tasks, roles and obligations are segregated between husband and wife, are most likely to belong to *closely* knit social networks outside the home. By contrast, *joint* conjugal relationships, about which so much has subsequently been written, are the products of a *loosely* structured social network, where husbands and wives, as individuals, are only weakly attached to groups based on work, leisure, neighbourhood or kin. Like the Bethnal Green studies, Bott's work demonstrated some of the interconnections between what goes on inside the family and the structural relations outside; in particular she was able to offer a model for understanding variations in the marriage relationship by reference not only to social class differences, but also to aspects of the wider social network.

These studies, along with those about 'affluent' workers (Goldthorpe et al. 1969) that we referred to in part 2, added further support to the belief that marriage in the decades after World War II had become more privatized, insular and cut off from broader social arrangements. A stereotype began to emerge in popular commentary, supported to some extent by the arguments of social scientists (Berger and Kellner 1964; Fletcher 1966), which saw 'modern' marriage as a product of the meeting of 'strangers', unaffected either by family preferences or membership of an existing network of friends, neighbours or kin. Changing patterns of higher education also influenced this phenomenon: the couple who meet while away at university and then go on to marry and live in some other part of the country, away from either set of parents, being the archetypal example. Thus social and geographical mobility could contribute to the rise of this style of marriage. Couples who have risen in the class structure or moved around the country might have little to gain psychologically, or even materially, from remaining close to both families of origin. They might therefore be especially conscious of creating a 'partnership' which is unique and individual and which places particular emphasis on the 'privacy' of their domestic arrangements.

The later work of Young and Willmott (1973) considerably expanded this thesis. In a study of 'work and leisure in the London region' they went on to argue that domestic life was indeed taking on new meanings and significance and that these changes were permeating throughout the social class structure. They argued that modern families, and particularly marital relationships within them, were becoming more 'symmetrical', characterized by both spouses in paid employment and an equal sharing of both the burdens of domestic labour and the pleasures of access to leisure. This pattern had emerged first in the upper middle classes and was now filtering inexorably down the social pecking order until the point where it would be 'enjoyed' by everyone. Although this study has been subject to very considerable criticism (Oakley 1974), it remains a very influential work, frequently appearing on the reading lists of counselling and social work training courses. Along with the Rapoports' study of dual career families (Rapoport and Rapoport 1976) it has also been widely used by popular commentators (Green 1984) as evidence of a sea change in marital norms and behaviour.

The reasons why such studies have acquired an influence way beyond their merits are complex and important. On the one hand their findings present a comforting picture of harmony and adaptability to the changed economic circumstances of the late 1950s and early 1960s. More significantly, their portrayal of contemporary marriage is very optimistic, conveying a move towards relationships which are more equal, rewarding and able to provide not only a considerable measure of material security, but also the potential for self-understanding and personal growth in partnership with one's spouse. For this latter reason in particular these sociological accounts demonstrate a syntonicity with therapeutic ideologies of marriage such as those developing around the same time within the marital agencies, and which we have already referred to as the predominant imagery of *Marriage Matters* (1979).

Paradoxically, one of the most influential factors contributing to the enhanced sense of privacy in marriage during this period, and subsequently, has been the increasing frequency and candour of *public* discussion about the meaning and purpose of sexuality. In relation to marriage, this meant the growing belief that 'successful' marriages were those in which 'good' sex was also to be found, and the acceptance that the *recreational* aspects of sexual activity had come to predominate over the *procreational*. But the freedom to explore such sexual territories could only be found in the context of the independent living and 'place of their own' which, as we have seen, couples had also come to expect. In this way, as Foucault (1979) has argued, marriage locates the partners' sexuality within a particular contemporary discourse, controlled not through prohibitions, but through the generation of diffuse sets of 'oughts' and expectations in which secrecy and privacy loom large. Thus while the 'private' inner core of couple relationships may protect many secrets, sex is likely to be regarded as *the* secret, the most private element of the relationship.

By such means the structural aspects of isolated contemporary marriage found their private, psychological correlates. It was this relationship, between the outer world of structure and the inner world of feelings, that provided the stimulus to a new generation of social researchers who became interested in marriage and domestic life during the 1970s and 1980s.

In the 1970s many empirical researchers with an interest in marriage and domestic life came under the influence of a theoretical perspective deriving from the *phenomenological* tradition. This had been particularly developed in the works of Schutz (1964), Berger and Luckman (1967) and Garfinkel (1967). Its defining characteristic was an attempt to elucidate the meanings of social situations and to describe the ways in which relationships and organizations are socially constructed through the purposive activities of individuals. One effect of this was to move the focus away from what people *do*, to what they *say* they do; for it is through language, conversation and interaction between persons that the social world is maintained. This in turn is made possible by a tacit obedience to innumerable and highly complex rules and agreements which govern human interaction; these constitute a delicate veneer of social order, which for most of the time is maintained, but which can easily be punctured, unwittingly or otherwise. We should of course remember that such theories are the product of a particular historical moment; the period from the late 1960s to mid-1970s saw a great preoccupation with issues of sexual politics and the critique of established moral and value systems. This was also the era of 'the happening', some spontaneous outbreak of bizarre behaviour in a public place, which beautifully illustrated the friability of 'normal' social relations. The spirit of the age was therefore about debunking, demythologizing and deconstructing the values and institutions of established society.

These ideas had major implications for marriage and family researchers and opened up whole new agendas of inquiry. Getting married, having children, making a home, going to work were all now to be seen as social accomplishments, not in the everyday understanding of that term, but in the sense of purposive activities which hour by hour, day by day, help create the social world and make possible what we uncritically refer to as 'normal family life'.

One way of understanding these processes is to look at situations in which 'normal family life' has been disrupted in some way. Margaret Voysey's (1975) study of families with a physically or mentally handicapped child provides a particularly good illustration of this. Her book *A Constant Burden*, with its interesting subtitle, *the reconstitution of family life*, is primarily concerned with the way parents come to terms with the reality of having a handicapped child. Voysey argues that any understanding of this experience must rest upon an analysis of *why*, when interviewed, parents say what they say; she suggests that the parents to whom she spoke tended to minimize the objective difficulties they experienced, emphasizing instead the essential normality of their family circumstances. For Voysey, such a tendency is consistent with parents' 'performances' in other semi-public settings, involving health care and social work personnel, when they are likely to be asked, albeit implicitly, to evaluate their performance as parents. To do so they must rely upon a repertoire of beliefs and theories about what constitutes 'normal' parenthood. We can learn from this that to study a 'problem' or 'anomalous' family situation is in part to uncover our ignorance about the social construction of 'ordinary' marriages and families, and indeed to call such categories totally into question.

Work of this kind therefore begins to draw together *social* theories about marriage and family life, which are primarily derived from research data, with *therapeutic* understandings, which are mainly inferred from clinical and practitioner experience. We would suggest that these two often overlap in the form of contemporary public moralities about marriage and family life which find their way into both popular and professional discourse. As we have tried to show, these public moralities are rooted in particular combinations of material and ideological change. One of their effects is to make marriage the locus of a wide range of economic, social and personal aspirations, a crucible with the potential for both achievement and failure. This makes the study of marriage, in its various guises and settings, of crucial importance.

METHODOLOGICAL PROBLEMS

This brings us to a number of concerns we have about the current state of methodology in marriage research, and in particular, issues surrounding the training and supervision of researchers. Our observations here are drawn from numerous discussions in which we have compared and contrasted the techniques used by both researchers and therapists in their work with couples.

Following in various ways the spirit of *phenomenological* inquiry which we have described, there is now a long list of recent studies which claim to adopt a perspective which allows couples and members of families to 'speak for themselves' and to 'tell their own story'. Within this tradition there are, for example, studies of parenting (Backett 1982); of fatherhood (Lewis 1986; Lewis and O'Brien 1987); of stepfamilies (Burgoyne and Clark 1984); of newly-weds (Mansfield and Collard 1988); of the effects of unemployment on families (Forster 1987); of grandparenthood (Cunningham-Burley 1987); and of the marriage relationship (Askham 1984), to name merely a handful. We believe these represent some of the most exciting recent developments in the study of marriage and family life in Britain. To varying degrees however they all raise questions about the most appropriate ways to conduct this kind of research: questions of method, of ethics and of confidentiality.

It has now become an accepted rhetoric among some researchers who favour qualitative methods to describe their approach to interviewing by such terms as 'open-ended' or 'in-depth'. By this they seek to distance themselves from the use of other, more positivistic methods, which rely on the collection of quantitative data which will be analysed statistically, and which will usually be collected by survey methods of one sort or another. The 'depth interview' has many attractions. It can be conducted with minimal preconceptions on the part of the interviewer, who may have only a vague set of hunches about the subject of inquiry. It can allow the respondent to determine the range and depth of the topics which are covered. It encourages openness, rapport, disclosure and other virtues which are conducive to the collection of 'rich' data. Above all perhaps, it is a method which allows the researcher simultaneously to collect *and* analyse the data. This makes it a *reflexive* technique which permits the reframing of questions and the checking out of hypotheses in the course of the data-gathering process. It allows what Ricoeur (1976) calls the 'hermeneutic circle' to be operationalized: the researcher begins with a set of fore-understandings of the subject, which is then explored in the course of the interview, this in turn produces reflections on the fore-understanding which cause the nature of the inquiry and the questions to be altered and modified. We can see that this form of interviewing is dynamic; it calls for swift thinking and adaptation on the part of the interviewer. It is also risky; if badly conducted it can create intellectual chaos out of the order of the social world and may produce unwelcome and unexpected reactions in the person being interviewed. This may be a particular risk when the subject of inquiry is some aspect of personal life, such as the experience of marriage, marital problems or divorce.

We find it a paradox therefore that social researchers who have so prized this method of working have paid so little attention to its consequences, both for the researchers and those who agree to take part in their studies; an exception at the time of writing is a useful paper by Brannen (1988). To our knowledge, this kind of work is frequently conducted by postgraduate students or by relatively junior and inexperienced research staff. These are most often selected for their academic track record or potential, rather than any proven skills or experience in interviewing, still less the personal qualities which may be essential in order to conduct work of this kind: openness, tolerance and the ability to empathize. It is worth contrasting these selection criteria with the carefully refined and evaluated procedures which have been developed in counselling agencies of various sorts. This point also holds for the levels of supervision which subsequently ensue. Whereas the counsellor's tutor will give priority to the personal and professional issues which will be raised both in training and in the counselling process, academic supervision will be much more orientated to the achievement of research goals. As a result, researchers can feel isolated, stressed and disturbed. They may be undertaking work which calls for great sensitivity, which makes them privy to many personal 'secrets' and frequently involves the exploration of painful aspects of a person's life. Most of these are likely to go unrecognized and unacknowledged by the research supervisor; regrettably, personal supervision does not yet have an acknowledged place within the culture of social research.

This point holds even more strongly in relation to *training*. Earlier in this part of the book we devoted considerable space to the question of training for marital work; we were forced to acknowledge that training is poorly developed and fairly difficult to obtain. For social researchers wishing to carry out marriage and family studies the situation is quite different: there is no training whatsoever. Indeed, it is only those, usually part-time and non-academic, workers, who are hired to carry out government and market research surveys who are likely to receive training or supervision at all. And this is simply in the interests of reliability and replicability. By contrast the 'professional', 'academic' researcher learns on the job, using an apprenticeship model which would have looked archaic in the nineteenth century. Social researchers are allowed to begin field work with the most meagre of personal and professional preparation. This is in stark contrast to the general situation in social work, counselling and psychotherapy, where even though generally agreed codes of prac-tice may not yet have been developed, there is considerable agree-ment about the degree of preparation which will be required before a worker begins to see clients. Far more would be expected of the volunteer marriage guidance counsellor by way of training and supervision than would ever apply to the professional, paid social researcher. We find this both worrying for those concerned and probably detrimental to the quality of the work which is undertaken.

Further problems are revealed when we look at the ways in which relationships are managed between researchers and researched. Many studies of this kind are based on what are known as opportu-nistic samples; they comprise volunteers, those who have agreed to take part as a result of personal contacts, 'snowballing' techniques and so on. This is an understandable response, since the very specific sets of personal and family circumstances which are of interest to researchers are often not accessible through conventional sampling routes. The absence of random samples in this work has to be accepted, and there are usually ways in which the researcher can exercise some degree of control over the recruiting process, so as to eliminate markedly atypical cases. More problematic are the kinds of research relationships which then ensue. There is a great tendency for researchers, especially when working with disadvantaged groups, to misjudge the degree of 'empathy' which is appropriate. This misjudgement can lead to a collusion between the two parties. Indeed this is often at the very heart of the respondents' willingness to take part. The researcher has come to hear 'their' story, to tell it like it is, to juxtapose it with media reports or the results of clinical research findings. Study members, perhaps aware of these other versions – particularly those in the press – may be willing to respond on this basis. Guaranteed anonymity, they may be highly motivated to give their account, to show for example, that single parents can 'cope', that stepfamilies can 'work' or that 'ordinary' people do divorce and remarry. The warning signs should already be in evidence, but the researcher, eager to gain trust and develop rapport, will be only too willing to ignore them. Not only will this create 'no go' zones in the subsequent interviews, when whole topic areas will be beyond discussion, it also illustrates the way in which apparently naturalistic accounts will have been heavily coloured by the implicit rules which already govern the interview. This is not because researchers forget Oakley's (1981) maxim that 'there can be no intimacy without reciprocity', but rather that they misjudge the form which that intimacy should take.

Further slippages and miscalculations can take place in the management of the subsequent interviews. The researcher is faced with problems of recordability, since the chief object of in-depth interviewing is to obtain verbatim accounts of what is said. The most common way of doing this is by audio recording, a method which has been greatly simplified in recent years by improvements in the available technology. Since this kind of work most often takes place in respondents' homes it is important to have recording methods which are portable and unobtrusive; this may be one of the reasons why video recording, a now accepted technique in family therapy and some clinical studies, is largely untried by social researchers. But however useful it may seem to tape record interviews in full, there are also potential dangers. There is a great temptation, for example, to let the interview run on unnecessarily. Loquacious respondents may be difficult to stop or interrupt and the open-ended format of the interview becomes a weakness. The knowledge that everything is being recorded, particularly when the respondent is eager to talk, can also discourage concentration on the part of the interviewer, who knows that everything said will be subsequently retrievable. In short, some of the dynamic properties of the interview disappear, and it begins to look increasingly like the structured questionnaire format which it is attempting to avoid. It is common, for example, to hear researchers talk about 'wonderfully rich' interviews which last four or five hours, and we know of at least one respondent who, seeing that the interviewer was tiring, offered to go on talking into her own machine and post the completed tape at a later date. We would contrast this sort of practice with the conventions of the 'therapeutic hour', and the belief, widely held by counsellors and therapists, that the optimal time period for work of this kind is, for all parties, 60 to 90 minutes.

Recordability can also be used by researchers as a reason for interviewing spouses separately, rather than together. Indeed, it is surprising when one surveys the sociological literature on marriage research to see how few studies have been carried out using couple interviews, Askham (1984) being a notable exception. It *can* be argued that such interviews are more difficult to record satisfactorily. They are probably more difficult to conduct, and this would seem to be a reason why researchers, like practitioners, often look for ways of separating the spouses in order that they can be interviewed separately. This is understandable, but regrettable. It is certain to lose many of the elements which studies of marriage are designed to elicit: qualities of interaction, modes of address, the social construction of the couple identity. On the other hand it can be argued that solo interviews allow greater freedom to spouses to express personal thoughts and feelings, and that they free each spouse to develop an individual view of what is not one, but *two* marriages. This is especially important when addressing issues of gender difference. It should be noted though that separate interviews can also create anxieties for spouses: 'What is he/she going to tell you that can't be said in front of me?' From experience we know that this can be particularly exacerbated when the spouse who is not being interviewed is around elsewhere in the home: 'What is going on in there, it seems to be taking a very long time . . .' This can also mean, where the first interview is lengthy, that the second one has to be rushed, or must be rearranged; in either case causing unnecessary anxiety for both respondent and researcher. And all of this in the context of home interviews where space, privacy and quiet may be at a premium.

A number of *ethical* problems also flow from this style of social research. We have seen that couples and families who take part in studies of this kind usually volunteer to do so, to some degree. They are under no obligation to participate, and will therefore decide to get involved for a variety of reasons. Sometimes this will be the altruistic belief that taking part will in some way 'help others', in the first instance maybe the hapless researcher, desperate to complete the study quota. Beyond that there may be some idea of helping those in a similar situation: those about to embark upon a particular change in their lives (for example, getting divorced or remarrying) or those requiring the support of helping professionals, who are by implication likely to make use of the study findings when published. It also seems clear from the experiences of a number of researchers that respondents often agree to take part out of unconscious motives to get something for themselves. Researchers in this field will be all too familiar with the interview which concludes with the respondent saying something like: 'Do you know, I've never told anybody all that before?' At one level this may be perfectly appropriate; the interview is a unique event with its own rules and boundaries. But on the other hand we are left feeling that something has been opened up on these occasions which has not been resolved. The interview may be a one-off, or part of a short series; it is unlikely that the personal consequences of taking part will have been discussed with the respondents either before or during the research process. So that personal issues which the researcher has been instrumental in raising are then left as the sole responsibility of the respondent, who must find some means of resolving them, or not. We believe that this is both unsatisfactory and unethical. Whatever the motivations of the respondents, research interviews should never be seen as a substitute for counselling or therapy, but neither should they be allowed to become a scientific equivalent of slash and burn agriculture: unlike the nomadic horticulturalist, the social researcher must take some responsibility for what is left behind.

This applies also to questions of confidentiality. It is common for researchers to secure the 'informed consent' of those taking part in their studies. As we have seen, this will be based at best on a partial understanding of what is going to take place. Likewise, respondents are usually fairly ill informed about what is likely to happen to the information they supply. They will be told, of course, that what they say will be kept confidential, that the data will only be available to members of the research team, that it will be impossible to link actual names and addresses to each respondent's file, that pseudonyms will be used in the final publication and so on. In most cases, all of this they will accept, usually with worryingly cavalier dismissals of being in any way concerned about such matters. How many respondents, we wonder, shrug off all of these reassurances by saying something like 'Well, we've got nothing to hide, you could go ahead and print our names in your book for all we care'? This of course is an unsatisfactory state of affairs. We might say that respondents owe it to themselves to be more responsible; but also people can change their position, particularly after the interviews have taken place and they have had some time to reflect on them. We also know, from painful experience, how even unwittingly, confidentialities can be breached in the desire to share findings, discuss cases with colleagues or whatever. Even the most attentive of researchers will be unable to say, in the long run, what is likely to happen to the data. Will the transcripts be kept, will the tapes be destroyed, is any of the data to be used for other types of analysis, stored in an archive or used for teaching purposes? It is rare when such questions can be answered with total confidence. That they are almost never asked by respondents is not the point.

Finally, there is the question of how this data is analysed. This is a very big subject, which we cannot properly tackle here, save to make one point which relates more to the practicalities of method than to the deeper issues of methodology. Most of the studies we have described, which use these sorts of open-ended, qualitative techniques, make use of relatively small study groups or samples. There is very little consensus on what constitutes a satisfactory number of cases, but available evidence suggests a range of between 20 and 60. It would be helpful to think this through a little more. One feature of this work is that it produces, even from fairly small numbers of cases, very large amounts of transcript data. This is unwieldy and difficult to analyse systematically; it is common for a lot of data to be produced which is not used. We would like to suggest that social researchers, particularly sociologists, develop more confidence in the use of case studies, where numbers are less important than the detailed explication of a particular set of experiences and circumstances. This would not only be cost effective, but would also free researchers from the need continually to seek comfort in the pseudo-positivistic inferences of ratios, proportions and trends.

We cannot here go too far in recommending possible solutions to these dilemmas. For the moment it is sufficient to point out that, even for its supporters, the qualitative methodology of open-ended, in-depth interviewing poses numerous problems. We hope, however, that these can be recognized and responded to, without detracting from the overall value of the method and its potential for development and wider application.

RESEARCH INTO MARITAL WORK

In parallel to the developments in qualitative studies of marriage and marital relationships, there has also emerged a corpus of inquiry which is more *evaluative* than *illuminative* in its purpose, because more focused on persons in trouble and seeking help in resolving their problems. In general, this work has been about the influence on practice of particular models or conceptual frameworks, about the characteristics of presenting problems, forms of intervention, client or patient expectations and issues in service organization and delivery. Some of this work has been in the qualitative tradition of research which we have described; some has sought to generalize from a few intensive studies of couples in treatment; some has been similar in kind to clinical trials conducted in medical and psychological research, though regrettably often without the controls necessary to proper comparative evaluations of different treatment methods. There have been attempts to link models of marriage with particular forms of intervention (Paolino and McCrady 1978), but the kind of information and evaluation which arises from sociological research has had relatively little impact on the practice of marital counselling or therapy. Compared to the situation in the United States, resources devoted to any kind of research on marital work in the United Kingdom have been very limited; but as we shall show, the position is improving.

In his important work *Marital Tensions*, subtitled *Clinical studies towards a psychological theory of interaction*, Dicks (1967) took as the first of the concepts on which his work was based 'The Social Setting' in which he explored the background (as he saw it) against which to view the great increase in marital stress and breakdown. We know from formal investigation (Haldane and McCluskey 1980a) and from continuing less structured inquiry, that this book has had a significant influence on the thinking and practice of a range of professionals. It is a major part of the history and development of the Tavistock Institute of Marital Studies in London, to the work of which we have already referred. In turn, it is evident that this history and practice significantly influenced the organization, content and proposals of the central government interdepartmental inquiry which led to *Marriage Matters*. That same year saw the publication from the Institute of a major inquiry (Mattinson and Sinclair 1979) into marital work in a local authority social services setting, a study which might find parallels not only today but also in other services and agencies. While there is some evidence to indicate that such research and reporting may eventually influence face-to-face practice, there is no evidence to show that it has materially influenced the organization and delivery of services.

Marriage Matters listed recommendations for five specific areas of research. These were: (1) case studies describing forms of presenting problem; (2) development studies showing how couples with particular kinds of marital problems present to specific agencies; (3) policy studies of the interaction between changes in marriage and the responses of the marital and other agencies; (4) epidemiological and social studies of the distribution and causes of marital problems in society; (5) organizational studies, focusing on the structures and dynamics of the marital agencies and their relationships with one another. These recommendations have had only a minimal response. This may be due to the somewhat arbitrary nature in which the topic areas are defined; it may be yet one more consequence of the fact that a very small minority of practitioners and organizers are also researchers, but it also assuredly relates to a lack of money invested in research. Indeed, a leader in *The Times*, published at the time of writing (1988), saw fit to comment:

> The denial of adequate funding for basic research into the causes of marriage breakdown would be justified only if it were known for certain, in advance, that such causes are in principle undiscoverable; or if it were known that, on being discovered, nothing could be done about them. Neither is true. Modest expenditure would be likely to produce significant progress. Numerous promising research avenues have not been explored, simply for lack of money.

In the late 1970s, a cohort of practitoners identifying research topics on work with couples gave priority to questions of treatment, selection, methods and outcome. Of 13 topics identified from the responses, the three most frequently mentioned were: effectiveness of treatment and outcome, evaluation and comparison of techniques, indications and contraindications for intervention (Haldane and McCluskey 1980b). To an increasing extent, research in marital work is focused on these concerns.

In 1969 the National Marriage Guidance Council established a research advisory board, which continued to 1988; members represented a range of disciplines and professions and under its auspices a number of studies were undertaken, of which we shall mention four. The study by de Groot (1985) of marriage counsellors in medical settings has already been referred to. In addition, Gaunt (1985) carried out interesting work on the importance of the first interview within the counselling process, with the significant finding that couples are more likely than lone clients to drop out of counselling after the first session. In a further study, Gaunt (1987) has monitored the use of reception interview schemes within marriage guidance and concludes that these are of considerable benefit, provided that they can be offered to the vast majority of clients at the first point of contact and that they can be followed up by a counselling appointment within a specified time period; she also makes recommendations about who should conduct the interviews and their form and duration. Finally, a detailed piece of research by Hunt (1985) contains a rich analysis of client expectations of the agency, paying particular attention to gender differences, and attempts to measure the extent to which expectations are being met, again making recommendations for changes in organizational policy. These studies show in a most encouraging way the kind of information and understanding which can be developed when practitioners are supported in their research by their own agency. It is perhaps too early, especially considering Relate's major reorganization since then, to evaluate the effect of these studies on the organization of training and services and on the practice of its counsellors.

There is extensive reference to research in Dryden's (1985) two-volume *Marital Therapy in Britain* and two chapters merit particular attention. In his overview of research on marriage in Britain, Chester (1985b) devotes a section to marital problems, discussing such topics as the incidence of troubled marriage; the association between problems and the duration of marriage, age at marriage, social class; the impact of children (or their absence) on the marital relationship; and violence in marriage. The interest of medical practitioners in the effect of mental or physical handicap – whether of child or parents – on marriage, along with psychiatry's contributions to research on alcoholism and marriage as well as psychopathology and marriage are mentioned only briefly in a paragraph on 'other topics of research' (1985b:250). It is not clear why this range of research is discussed in this way, other than that its literature is described as 'too scattered and diverse for review' (1985b:26); but we agree with Chester that this kind of work is usually insulated from marriage research in the social sciences. In the second volume, Hooper (1985) presents an overview of research in marital therapy, not quite half of which focuses on such research in Britain. He contrasts the significance of British practitioners' contributions to theory (particularly psychodynamic theory) about marital relationships with the dearth of empirical research. British research is reviewed under the headings of sex therapy, client experience studies, marital work in a social service setting and marital therapy in connection with specific problems. We strongly support Hooper's assertion of the need to develop marital work in primary care settings, where the highest number of marital problems is likely to be presented, in whatever guise.

In the past much research on marital work has been devoted to comparing one with another the various models or conceptual frameworks (some of which we referred to in part 3) or to arguing the unequivocal merits of a particular approach. These comparisons have been too general, too global, and reports of how much better one model for practice is than another often ignore important variants. That one approach is as good as another or that it does not matter which approach one uses, are both unsafe statements, but as it becomes appreciated that each has something useful to add to the corpus of knowledge and to the potential for effective practice, so has the focus of research been shifting. The move has been towards the attempt to match particular methods to particular kinds of problems presented by couples, a trend more evident in the behavioural and systems approaches and still relatively crude, but a significant step forward. It is not yet clear whether there is a development towards an approach which integrates various conceptual frameworks or whether the emphasis is on pragmatism.

A recent commentary on research, practice and organization in relation to marital therapy (Haldane 1988) shows that the couples studied present problems which seem often far removed from the severity and complexity of those encountered in the course of everyday clinical practice. Models and approaches to therapy seem rarely applied in unmodified form. Treatment methods and procedures are rarely described in detail. Follow-up is measured more often in terms of weeks than of months or years. The criteria for evaluation of treatments insufficiently represent the proposals or expectations of the spouses involved. Much of the literature is out of touch with the real concerns of patients, clients, practitioners. It is a literature which largely ignores the rich vein of sociological commentary on contemporary marriage which we have been describing. The need to take account of the work of other professionals is shown by Gorell Barnes (1987) in an extensive review, particularly of the work of Rutter and his colleagues, which indicates that a range of studies focusing on child development, child behaviour and parenting, has direct application to methods of working with families and couples. Despite these limitations, research is leading to an emerging consensus of opinion about how best to resolve some of the problems and choices in marital work, how most effectively to intervene and with what aims. This note of cautious optimism influences our comments in the final part of the book.

5

Consultation about Marriage

It is important to point out that the entire field of practice, research and organization which we have been describing and exploring here is historically a very recent phenomenon. The history of the marital agencies in Britain spans but half a century, and social research into marriage has developed only in the second half of that period. As a society, our concern better to understand the nature of the marriage relationship and to *problematize* it in particular ways, is very recently developed. Although there has been identifiable public concern since before World War II about the 'breakdown' of the institution of marriage, the concepts and terminology of counselling and therapy have established themselves in popular discourse much more recently. It was not until the mid-1970s that there was sufficient impetus for an interdepartmental government inquiry into these areas, leading eventually to the recommendations of *Marriage Matters*. As we have seen however, there has been very little response to these recommendations. Agreement is lacking about the most effective models for intervention. Training for both researchers and practitioners is seriously limited. There seems little prospect of any major development of services, whether statutory or voluntary.

With recurring evidence of these limitations, it has been tempting at times to shift our focus from *marriage* to a wider discussion of family and domestic life. Particularly when looking at the sociological literature it is hard to avoid getting caught up in wider debates about families and households; however we have tried to explore such issues only in so far as they cast light on the relationship and institution of marriage, recognizing that marriages are highly interconnected with the material and ideological structures which surround them. Similarly, it is tempting to look to methods and procedures developed in the field of family therapy when seeking to overcome some of the current difficulties in marital work; we are aware, for example, of pressure from some quarters to abandon working with couples in favour of a systems-based approach which focuses ideas about cause and possibilities for change on the entire nexus of family relationships. Our preference is to resist such pressures, in the belief that adult couple relationships should be granted a considerable measure of autonomy and cannot be seen as artefactual subsystems of family life. To take this latter view, indeed, seems to us to reveal a rather uncritical acceptance of particular ideologies of 'marriage' and 'the family' as phenomena inevitably and inextricably linked to one another. It is important to recognize that for some, being married may not lead inexorably to parenthood, and indeed that having children and being part of a 'family' does not have to be predicated on formal, legally constituted marriage. So while no one can dismiss the social significance of various forms of household and family living arrangements, or indeed dyadic alternatives to heterosexual marriage, our concern here has been principally with that relationship which in our society is constituted as the formal, legal and publicly recognized *marriage* of a woman and a man.

This particular form of wedlock, which at one level seems to attract so much public attention, is as we have shown, still rather poorly understood by researchers and practitioners. It has become almost a commonplace to acknowledge that marriage must be seen as a phenomenon which is *both* public and private, institutional and relational, structural and psychological. These are useful distinctions, helpful in the task of defining different aspects of marriage, but less so in demonstrating how each might engage with the other as interrelated aspects of a complex whole. In this respect, the concept of boundaries and transactions across them can be helpful. In part 3 we discussed how such concepts or metaphors can be useful in consultative work with couples. Here we wish to define an area of potential interest to both researchers *and* practitioners.

In a sense, marriage is about transactions across boundaries: the boundary between unconscious and conscious worlds, between one person and another, between the couple and their children, between couple and the world outside their intimate affairs. These boundaries must be to a sufficient degree open if interaction is to take place, if change is to be possible, if one is to be known to the other. In a sense, marriages are constituted out of the minutiae of everyday existence: from eating, drinking, doing the housework, cooking and shopping, to making love, talking and playing with the children, deciding 'what to do', worrying about paying the latest bill. It is not difficult to imagine a boundary around this micro-world, this private reality, this area into which intrusion can be unwelcome. In this relatively closed world choices are made, and there is potential for freedom of expression, personal development and satisfaction. Outside the boundary lies the public dimension of marriage. Here the minutiae of daily marital relationships are overtaken by configurations of rules, norms, values and laws relating to marriage. On one side of the boundary, dialogue, collaboration and mutual understanding are essential to maintaining the relationship. On the other, exhortation and speech-making risk persons becoming stereotypes. Daily life for husband and wife means constant transactions back and forward, in and out, through these boundaries. These boundaries are in a sense also identity-defining and potentially helpful defensive systems, creating the possibility for development in the lives and relationship of the couple which is neither purely individualistic nor wholly social in its determinants. The nature and experience of transactions across the private-public boundary deserves to be better understood by both researchers and practitioners and should form an important part of our thinking about research and intervention in marriage.

5.1 Marriage, Marital Problems and Social Policy

Whether as researcher or as practitioner, the more we consider marriage, the more we have to point out its contradictions and paradoxes. In the second half of the twentieth century to marry in our culture has become a near-universal experience of adult life. Despite increased rates of cohabitation; despite higher rates of divorce; despite more vocal, open and organized gay and lesbian communities pronouncing themselves antithetical to traditional norms about marriage; despite the attacks from feminism and the left, marriage continues to hold a central place within the normative structure of our society. Whatever views to the contrary we may hold at different points in our lives, most of us decide to marry at some stage. And the majority remain married to the same person for a lifetime. We might conclude from this that a great deal would be known about marriage. Given its crucial role within the value system, its centrality within a nexus of interlocking beliefs about home, domesticity and parenthood, its importance to the moral guardians of church and state, we might expect greater attention to have been given to it by researchers. And yet it still remains marginal to studies in the social sciences; in sociology in particular having been for long regarded as an insignificant and 'soft' area of study, it has re-emerged in recent years, but frequently as a mere adjunct to studies of gender, power or material divisions within households. Marriage appears as a phenomenon which its detractors dismiss as not meriting focused study and which its supporters find embarrassing to expose to public scrutiny. The institution of marriage is all around us, there appears to have been a growing preoccupation over a long period with the significance of the marriage relationship, and yet the research community remains ignorant about so many aspects of married life.

This contradictory situation, of knowledge and ignorance, wanting to know and being unable to make a commitment, is often mirrored or replicated in the marital relationship itself. There likewise, opposing attitudes or experiences or feelings are held in tension, often painfully. For many husbands and wives a problem expressed as a difficulty in conveying intimate thoughts or feelings to a consultant can be an extension of a fear of being better known and understood by the spouse and of having to take the consequences of this. As one husband said: 'It would be a help if she understood me better, but do I really have to tell her all about myself?' Some couples talk readily about 'the marriage' or 'our marriage' as if it were a relationship outside themselves, of which they are not part. Some couples have no difficulty in talking about marriage, especially rights and responsibilities, but do not often talk to each other, far less seek to know something of the other's experience of the relationship. To reveal and to know can be a burden; wife to consultant: 'But if I were to start to tell you what it's really like, where would that all end and what would you do with it?'

Ironically, there is a sense in which we know more about the category of phenomena labelled *marital problems* than we do about marriage more generally. We noted earlier, for example, that with the exception of some rather arid North American studies, there has been little inquiry into marriages which continue, where couples do not seek the help of marital agencies and which in ordinary terms might be variously described as 'happy', 'successful', 'good' marriages. What do such phrases mean? We appear to invest them with a good deal of significance, and yet we find them so hard to elaborate, whether in sociological, psychological or therapeutic terms. By contrast we do know something about the range of terms by which couples describe difficulties or distress in a marriage. We know that it is rare for couples to accept joint responsibility in the causes or development of the problem they bring for resolution. The difficulties between husband and wife are rarely at that stage seen as mutually constructed. More often the problem is 'him' or 'her'. By contrast, accounts of marital break-up given by those who go on to find and marry another spouse tend to emphasize, with hindsight, the relational rather than the individual aspects of the problem. But in general we still live in a culture where matrimonial causes, though no longer enshrined in law, have a clear reality in the minds of couples.

In several places earlier in the text we have referred to the question of blame. We have noted that spouses tend to see someone or something else as responsible for, as the cause of or to blame for the complained-of marital problem. Any one of a range of persons or situations may be seen as culpable: the other spouse or another person (such as a mother-in-law) or an event (bereavement or unemployment). In our society some 50 years ago, grounds for divorce were legally founded in causes or offences, such as cruelty or adultery, which became too readily seen as the behaviour which was 'to blame' for the marital distress. While such attitudes or explanations can be seen as unrealistic or simplistic, they nevertheless express a fundamental feature of personal relationships. 'It was him', 'it's not my fault', 'she's to blame', 'it's nothing to do with me'; these are phrases which belong to the language of persons from childhood to old age. They express a difficulty in acknowledging appropriate responsibility for problems in relationship and are the everyday evidence of denial. Is it possible that the inadequacies and limitations of statutory and voluntary services; the difficulties which spouses and couples have to overcome before finding responses appropriate to their needs, might also, in social terms, express similar dynamics? That the lives of couples are private; that their problems are their own concern; that the responsibility for creating change in their relationship must rest with them: such views can be articulated as demonstrations of positive concern. Alternatively, they can mean a rejection of all responsibility by others; a wish to keep such painful matters both private and hidden. If couples have only themselves to blame for difficulties in their marriages and only they can produce change, what need is there for responsive services? The possibility that others, that we in our membership of society, may share some of this blame, need not necessarily mean that this will be transmitted into concerned action; it may be one kind of reason for a resistance to increasing the possibilities for intervention.

In part 2 we suggested that the subject of 'marital problems' should be approached with extreme caution. These 'problems' embody the paradoxes and contradictions of marriage itself. They are to an extent ideological products of moral and professional groups which have successfully delineated and defined a category of phenomena. To that extent they are invested with an objective reality which can only be maintained by constant attention, reformulation and redefinition. Seen sociologically, marital problems, in the words of one of the popular rhetorics about marriage, need to be 'worked at'; they have not appeared of their own accord nor will they remain a social category by mere inertia. None of which, of course, is to deny or seek to explain away their reality at a subjective, interpersonal level. In part 3 we saw in more detail what this might mean, the power of marital distress to produce further problematic aspects in the lives of those involved. In part 4 we examined some of the organizational contexts in which couples might seek help with problems in marriages; from that we concluded that help is not easily available to couples in marital distress.

Marital problems, however defined, are generally acknowledged to be widespread in our society. Measured solely in terms of the divorce figures, hundreds of thousands of women and men are affected annually; it is reasonable to assume that those who obtain a divorce are only a portion of those experiencing difficulties at any given time. And yet there is a great reluctance on the part of professionals to work with these difficulties. Doctors, social workers, ministers of religion, do not appear to be much engaged in working with couples distressed in their marriages. Workers in the caring professions are certainly likely to be in regular contact with persons experiencing marital difficulties; but their response is often, in effect, one of avoidance. In most cases it seems preferable to choose *not* to work with marital problems, but to focus on something else – an illness, disability, a housing or financial problem – without exploring the relationship between the marital and other problems, without considering which is symptom and which is cause. Our experience is of professionals not wishing to get involved in this work, yet acknowledging that a major issue does exist. This seems to be a recurrent theme at conferences on marriage, where workers frequently explain that they are regularly in contact with clients or patients in marital difficulties, and yet are unable to become involved. The reasons are manifold: other pressures on their time, or lack of adequate training, or because wives say their husbands will not attend, or because they consider that marital problems cannot be given priority, or that only couples themselves can resolve their difficulties. And some go on to talk of how stressful an experience it can be to work with couples. One general practitioner, a competent clinician and much liked by his patients: 'I'll try my hand at almost anything, but God preserve me from married couples. We need a counsellor here.'

There is now considerable public acknowledgement that divorce rates in our society constitute a major social problem, at a variety of levels. We showed earlier that marriage break-up can affect the health of those involved; it creates difficulties in relation to questions of child custody and parental access; it appears to take a massive psychological toll, affecting wellbeing, work performance, the ability to build new relationships. We saw also that it is followed in a large proportion of cases by remarriage, in which the risks of a subsequent divorce are considerably increased. Even the most relativistic of sociologists could not 'explain away' the genuinely problematic nature of much of this, the wide extent of the problems and the ways in which they intermesh individual and structural dimensions. And yet, as we have seen, services offering specialized help with marital problems, with the personal (rather than the legal) aspects of divorce and with remarriage remain almost nonexistent in the statutory sector. Such help as is offered seems to be the product of local initiatives, individual interests and a willingness to engage in work which is regarded more generally as something to be avoided, or too complex to allow worthwhile intervention.

Why services offering marital counselling have remained so unequivocally a part of the voluntary sector is an interesting question, important in itself and also in what it may reflect of priorities in the statutory services. Is it perhaps because the relatively limited public profile of the voluntary agencies and the nature and settings of their premises allow the problems of marriage to remain largely hidden, unacknowledged and off the public agenda? Until fairly recently, the voluntary marriage counselling agencies have preferred to develop their activities quietly and unobtrusively, and their work has barely been open to public scrutiny or evaluation. As voluntary agencies only partly financed by central and local government funds, the extent to which this work has been monitored by government departments has been limited. Since *Marriage Matters* there have been a number of attempts to evaluate the work of the marital agencies, inspired mainly by the expansion of the services over the past decade. But such evaluation raises enormous questions about aims, what constitutes success and how it can be described, far less measured. Some of these questions can be resolved only when the agencies concerned become clearer about their models of *intervention*, which in turn depends upon the definition of a model or models of marriage. Do the marriage guidance services still wish to foster a particular set of values, principles and behaviours relating to marriage? Do they still wish actively to *promote* marriage within our society, as an institution believed to be fundamental to its wellbeing and stability and from which other desirable qualities may flow? Is their role to be seen within a treatment or service delivery model as offering a highly skilled, non-judgemental, focused response to those experiencing difficulties in their marriage? Will development in their work include what is presently called divorce counselling and conciliation? These are questions which the voluntary agencies will continue to explore, but which will not readily be resolved.

No doubt part of the difficulty lies in the lack of support, from any political quarter, for the work of the marital agencies. Is there some explanation for the fact that in the area of political debate and formulation of social policy marital problems are, at best, peripheral to the concerns of those who seek to determine provisions? There has in recent years been a good deal of political rhetoric about the family (usually by implication the nuclear family); about its importance for social stability; its role in nurturing and care-giving; its function in preventing crime or abuse; but there has been little public debate about marriage. Likewise, the growing concern of politicians and policy-makers over such issues as child abuse, violence, poverty, poor housing and unemployment has been addressed usually in structural or environmental terms. There seems to be a great reluctance to link these phenomena to the psychological worlds of those concerned. How to relate such issues to marital problems, in terms of either cause or effect, is a complex matter constantly at risk of being oversimplified; but that they are associated is not a matter for serious doubt. Despite all of the evidence in support of such an assertion, politicians seem reluctant to address the world of adult relationships, holding firmly to the fiction of the state's neutrality in the personal affairs of its citizens. Is it particularly difficult for those who live, move and act in the public arena openly to explore and risk exposing to wider scrutiny the problems which exist in intimate heterosexual relationships? Government policy in Britain in the 1980s successfully avoided such complex questions, by rigid adherence to a rule of nonintervention in the internal workings of voluntary organizations, coupled with an insistence that they should become less reliant on state finance and more self-supporting.

5.2 Consulting about Research and Intervention

We now turn to a consideration of ways of *developing* research and intervention in marriage, keeping in mind the kinds of contradictions and paradoxes we have been exploring and the need for more effective links between *practice, research* and *organization.* We believe that researchers and practitioners must be more receptive to one anothers' concerns, willing to exchange theories, methods and skills, and prepared at times to suspend disbelief about the others' underlying assumptions and philosophies. This process, to be worthwhile, must also be seen in terms of the organizational contexts in which research and intervention are carried out. We are not seeking to be prescriptive in our discussion of these matters, though we are conscious of the need for a full debate on the issues, involving a wide spectrum of professions and organizations.

As we have shown, in our society, marriage and its problems are subject to a variety of definitions. Attempts have been made to address marital problems in terms of a medical model couched in the language of aetiology, symptoms, treatment and cure. From this perspective the world of relationships is seen as a 'natural' realm, prone to dysfunction, but admissible of intervention on the part of skilled helpers. In professional terms these are usually psychiatrists, clinical psychologists or psychotherapists working with persons called 'patients'. Social work ideology and practice offers an alternative view; while it may draw on assumptions about attachments, bonding and loss which are rooted in the analytic tradition, it also locates these experiences in the practical and material world. Social work offers help to persons called 'clients'; it combines the skills of active listening and support with knowledge and advice about practical and material issues, such as welfare benefits, housing or community care. Those whose model for working with marital problems is primarily derived from counselling, adopt still another approach. Eschewing the medical model and perhaps sceptical about the extent to which practical social work help merely deals with the symptoms, rather than the causes, of marital difficulties, counsellors offer help which focuses on the problems of persons in relationship. This grants considerable autonomy to the individual, who is 'enabled' in the counselling process to make choices, to distinguish between courses of action, to explore the underlying feelings which shape behaviour. All of these approaches to marital problems have been criticized by sociologists. The medical model grants too little autonomy to the individual, since we are not mere slaves to our human physiology. The counselling model, by contrast, is idealistic and assumes levels of autonomy which are impossible to maintain in the external world. Social work merely reproduces the deep structural inequalities which exist in our society and is likely to engender a sense of personal responsibility or guilt in those whom 'the system' has treated unjustly. Better then, say sociologists, to construct *marriage* as the problem and examine the ways in which the norms, values and rules which surround it serve to create difficulties for particular categories of person, according to such factors as gender, age or social class.

To accept these positions risks a continued clinging to the oppositional rhetorics we referred to in part 1. Our task therefore should be to identify a way in which they can be transcended in order that new forms of understanding and thinking about marriage can be developed. Such developments should be capable of application by practitioners, researchers and managers, not as the expression of some all-embracing integrated theory, but as a way of thinking, communicating, acting which recognizes common ground and gives priority to collaboration and learning. Our approach is predicated on the assumption that intervention and research in marriage, and the organizations which undertake such work, can and should be developed beyond their present rather limited field of operation. The approach we seek to promote we have called *consultation*. In a paper with Una McCluskey (Haldane, McCluskey and Clark 1986) we developed the idea of consultation as both a perspective on marriage and as a model for action. Our perspective had three dimensions: sociological, psychodynamic and existential. We have been able to develop these various dimensions at different points in this book. They are clearly not capable of integration as such, though when juxtaposed, used creatively and with a measure of pragmatism, they can suggest solutions and ways of approaching particular problems. In combining these dimensions we have sought to draw out those aspects of marriage which are predicated on questions of gender, social class or age; we have looked to the way in which they relate to changing values about marriage, to changing beliefs and expectations. We have seen that these form part of a much wider process of social change. In this context persons, over the life course, are engaged in the process of making and breaking affectional bonds. The marriage relationship may draw on early childhood experiences, may be influenced by the characteristics of the marriages of the spouses' parents and will certainly be shaped by the influence of the unconscious on action. It will also provide a context in which existential realities may be addressed: concerns about the meaning, nature and purpose of existence, about being and becoming, about marriage as a place for self-actualization, for personal and joint development. That perspective and model have been explored and expanded in part 3, in which intervention in marriage was the primary focus. In the remainder of this final part we want to consider how some of these ideas about consultation may be related to developments in research and practice.

In earlier sections, when reviewing the development of research on marriage in this country, we saw how research concerns have often mirrored wider presuppostions about marriage within the culture, such as in the preoccupation with 'companionate' marriage at a time of general debate on the 'decline' of the extended family. Little formal research into marriage has been practitioner-led, in the sense of starting from the preoccupations and every day concerns of those working in the marital agencies. There has been little consultation about how research should develop in this area. Despite the existence of outside expertise, most of the evaluation studies which have been carried out, such as those described in part 4, have been conducted by personnel from within the agencies concerned. Since the publication of *Marriage Matters* there has only been one sustained forum in which researchers and practitioners have come together for an exchange of concerns and expertise, the Rugby Seminars, promoted by the National Marriage Guidance Council from 1979 to 1986. In general terms the political climate of Britain in the 1980s has not proved congenial to those interested in either marriage research or the evaluation of marital work. This is not merely because the relevant recommendations of *Marriage Matters* have failed to materialize; it is a direct statement about the day-to-day difficulties of sustaining and funding such work in a social context which is at best indifferent, and at worst openly inimical, to the whole field of activity.

It is perhaps not surprising therefore that a situation continues in which two areas of research endeavour lead largely independent lives. On the one hand, social researchers, mainly sociologists and/or feminists, have developed studies of marriage, divorce and remarriage. These have ranged from the socio-demographic detailing of major trends in marital behaviour to small-scale micro-studies of the intimate world of marriage. On the other hand, practitioners, partly we believe motivated by funding anxieties, have begun to engage in studies which monitor and evaluate their work, for example by testing the effectiveness of certain procedures in offering appointments, or examining expectations of the agency's clients, or exploring how the service can be developed in new settings, such as general practice. For most of the time there seems to be little cross-fertilization or overlap between the work of 'researchers' and 'researcher-practitioners'.

Yet each can learn from the other. In our opinion there is still a reluctance to develop research in counselling organizations; a feeling seems to persist that research may lead to academic qualifications for those who conduct it, but that it has little pay-off at the grass roots, where the 'real' work is going on. This may, of course, be born out of anxieties about exposing one's practice to dispassionate scrutiny, either individually or collectively. More fundamentally, we think it reflects a reluctance in counselling organizations to address cognitive issues. Where training and practice emphasize the dynamics of human relations, give prominence to feelings and emotions and prioritize notions of individuality and uniqueness, then it is understandable that there will be a reluctance to consider other approaches, especially those which look for patterns, similarities and trends. But there is no doubt that a knowledge of such trends can assist in strategic planning and policy formulation. It can also be of value to the individual worker in his or her practice, not least in better informing practitioners about the social context of their clients' lives. When linked to more broadly based work on marriage it can also enhance understanding of the ways in which *some* aspects of the clients' problems may be socially constructed. A better appreciation of this issue could lead in turn to more realistic formulations of what is achievable within the chosen model of intervention.

Conversely, as our criticisms in part 4 imply, researchers conducting work which is mainly reliant on qualitative methods can learn a great deal from the methods of training, supervision and intervention which have been developed by practitioners doing marital work. It is certainly necessary to pay far more attention to the question of selecting workers to do qualitative research with couples, and having done so to provide appropriate training, support and supervision, recognizing that such work may raise personal issues for those who undertake it. Researchers can learn a great deal from the skills which have been developed by practitioners. These would include refinements in the methodology of interviewing couples, something which has been largely ignored by marriage researchers, many of whom have chosen to see spouses individually, a technique which may have some merits, but which by itself certainly contributes to a loss of understanding of the couple relationship. It is quite clear that social researchers need to develop further their skills in 'contracting' with their respondents, an issue we explored at length in part 3 when considering the relationship between couple and consultant. This would include far greater attention than is commonly given to questions of confidentiality, how the interviews will be conducted, who will have access to the research data and how it will be used. We are advocates here of a more *consultative* approach on the part of researchers, who must accept considerable responsibility for raising with study participants the importance of such ethical issues, even in situations where the participants may appear initially to be rather dismissive of them. We have described in part 3 the role and responsibility of the consultant as container and manager of the holding environment in which the interview can be successfully accomplished. It is our view that the researcher working within such a consultative framework has similar responsibilities. As in the case of the therapist-consultant, the researcher-consultant must take responsibility for maintaining the space in which the interview takes place, for time-keeping and for engaging with the concerns of respondents about the implications of their taking part in the exercise. We would prefer to see smaller-scale studies, involving fewer participants, carefully conducted according to consultative principles, in preference to unintentionally positivistic efforts where the research falls between the methodologies of sample survey and phenomenological inquiry.

Beyond these issues of technique lie more fundamental questions about how the agenda for research into marriage is determined. We have already noted that this is a field where resources have been scarce, where work has often been conducted by individuals working in relative isolation and where lack of collaboration between disciplines, indeed the absence of any significant contact, has been only too evident. Collaborative efforts which have been made, such as those between historians and feminists (Lewis 1986), reveal the rich potential of joint work on marriage. At the moment we see the research of demographers, historians, feminists, sociologists and practitioners resting side by side in relative isolation. Individuals must take greater personal responsibility for working across these boundaries, and institutions must encourage them to do so. We remain staunchly committed to the recommendations of *Marriage Matters* on interdisciplinary work, though pessimistic about the extent to which it is achievable in the present climate. Certainly government departments and research councils are doing little to encourage such initiatives.

We have maintained throughout that the work of practitioners and researchers involved with marriage must be seen in its organizational context. We have also noted that organizations concerned principally with marital research are very few in number and that those dedicated solely to marital work are found only in the voluntary sector.

Only two relatively small and London-based organizations are committed to the provision of a service for couples, combined with the development of research and training programmes: the Tavistock Institute of Marital Studies and the Marriage Research Centre. Both of these continue to struggle for financial survival. Like the voluntary marital agencies they are confronted by the irony of a political and moral climate in which some primacy is given to concerns about marriage and family life, but where this is not matched by any sustained governmental support for the development of their work. Like so many other agencies in the fields of health, education and social welfare they are forced into the arena of the market economy and are under pressure to adopt fund-raising strategies more familiar to the world of commerce, marketing their services as if they were goods for sale. This is not a fertile environment in which to develop more consultative forms of working, which will allow boundaries to be crossed, disciplinary perspectives to be re-evaluated and new joint initiatives to emerge. But it is the climate in which organizations are now expected to operate and to that extent it cannot be ignored.

It seems to us unlikely that the present balance of responsibilities for marital work – resting between the voluntary and statutory sectors – will change fundamentally in the coming years. There is little sign of a commitment to the development of marital work in either medicine or social work. The activities of the voluntary marriage guidance councils do however appear to be expanding in scope and range. There has also been in recent years the emergence of an important new service offering opportunities for conciliation between couples who have divorced or are in the process of doing so. This is encouraging, though the development of the conciliation services remains patchy and halting. So what possibilities exist for consultation and development, and what forms might these take? We should like to suggest some possible areas.

While we do not have accurate data on the proportion of couples who have problems which they cannot resolve on their own, we do know that even among those who seek help there are difficulties in finding an appropriate agency. Our suspicion, though we do not yet have the evidence to support it, is that the service which any particular couple eventually find, will be in part a reflection of their position within the social class structure. A major issue for the future is therefore whether we need to train more people in the expertise of marital work, or whether there are less costly and perhaps more effective ways of providing help to those who need and seek it. We have already talked of two 'classes' of experts: those such as doctors, social workers and psychologists, who develop the necessary skills as part of their professional competence; and those such as marriage guidance counsellors, who offer their particular range of skills as part of a personal and organizational *raison de'être*. Our view is that there should be increased priority given to the training in marital work of personnel who are likely in their daily work to meet individuals, or couples, or families, who could be helped by the kind of approaches we have described. Doctors, social workers, psychologists, should not need to train as marriage guidance counsellors or psychotherapists before feeling confident to work in this way. We do not deny that some individuals should go on to develop further expertise, or that there is a place within our society for the voluntary marital agencies. Rather we emphasize that skills in marital work should become part of the basic competence of key professionals in the statutory services which offer some form of primary care. Of course this is too simple a scenario. Accepting always that some workers will become more experienced, more competent, more skilled than others, is there a place for the development of an identifiable, distinct profession of marital counsellors or therapists with a formal career structure? We think not, but many will disagree with this view. And who will in future be entitled to call themselves marital therapists or counsellors or consultants? There is at present in the United Kingdom an active debate among a wide range of psychotherapeutic and counselling organizations about acceptable standards of training and practice, ethical standards, guidelines and registration. The results of this debate – and there is increasing agreement on the basic questions – will undoubtedly affect the nature and organization of marital work. We would expect training and practice to be improved as a result, but that does not mean that organization and delivery of services to couples will also improve.

There is a further issue, about which we have so far said very little and which further reflects the complexities of providing services to couples, and that is the question of payment for help. So far at least, those who approach the statutory services seeking relief from their marital problems do not pay the doctors, social workers, psychologists for the services which they or their organizations provide. Nor is it likely for the time being that those professionals have costed the work involved. The fiction that such services are free is readily maintained. On the other hand, those who organise the marriage guidance services are increasingly aware of their cost, especially as grants from central and local government diminish. So clients are now being asked to contribute to costs; though at what rate, and for precisely which services, is still unclear. Should there be a scale of charges, a means testing? Who is to introduce this subject to clients: the counsellor at the first meeting, or is some more indirect method preferred, such as a discreet card passed to the client on leaving? A donation to a charity is one thing, payment for services another; but how to define each and how to contrast them? To seek payment may be seen as inconsistent with the voluntary status of counsellors, but there are growing pressures for counsellors to be paid employees of the marriage guidance services. How to explain all this to clients, donors, sponsors and government?

There are a number of other possible approaches most, so far as we are aware, untried. We have not come across any examples, for instance, of self-help groups of men, women or couples specifically organized to assist one another in the resolution of marital problems. Is this because such problems are still too private, too secret, too terrible to be subject to even limited public scrutiny? If so, this would be in contrast to problems around HIV infection, alcohol and substance abuse, incest, sexual assault, or mental illness and handicap. An increasing range of problems in behaviour and relationships is now thought amenable to such mutual support and succour; what is it about marital problems that prevents or disallows such a response? Is it possible that such groups could be formed if personnel trained in marital work and consultancy were to offer to help promote them and remain available for consultation as they develop? Perhaps one major barrier to the development of groups of this kind is that they tend to be linked to organizations which have a wider concern with 'marriage enrichment' and what is sometimes called 'marital wellness'. As such they appear to be caught up with the promotion of a particular ideology of marriage; this would seem to place powerful constraints on their ability to develop as a service which is widely available and easily made use of.

These questions are linked in turn to approaches predicated on notions of community development. Alongside the increasing bureaucratization and centralization of services within our society there are also movements to empower groups within local communities, encouraging them to identify and develop services relevant to local needs. Community approaches are being used successfully in a number of areas, including housing provision, health promotion, adult education and youth services. So far there do not appear to have been many such initiatives in marital work, though we know they are being experimented with by Relate, National Marriage Guidance. Of course there are already the Citizens' Advice Bureaux, legal aid offices and centres organized by local authorities and voluntary agencies which offer information and assistance with regard to rights and entitlements. But to our knowledge, there are no centres where *in the same place* wives or husbands can seek information, assessment or help about legal, financial, personal and health problems in marital relationships. Of course, it may be that in the current social, economic and political climate, marital problems may be regarded as too private or idiosyncratic to make such services worthwhile. Yet it may be that such developments would be viable if they were created out of a process of consultation with local communities and groups.

There has been a growing emphasis within the health services in recent years on the role of prevention rather than cure, on health promotion rather than curative medicine. It is not uncommon to hear those involved in marital work draw attention to similar concerns; given the relative failure to meet the needs of those experiencing marital problems, should not such limited resources as are available be diverted into preventive and educational strategies, rather than so-called 'remedial' work? There is to our knowledge currently no evidence that programmes of education or preparation for marriage have any significant long-term effect, notwithstanding the model or models of marriage which may be in use. Where they exist, indeed, they do appear to be linked with very particular sets of values surrounding marriage, such as those adopted by certain churches. Their applicability in more secular contexts, such as school or college education, is therefore relatively unknown. It is our view that given the present state of knowledge, we must give priority to providing services for those currently experiencing problems in their marital relationships.

This is not the same as saying that priority be given to those in *crisis*, those who feel urgently in need of finding help in resolving what has become an intolerable problem. There is a parallel here with the health and social services in which for so long priority has been given to acute illness and personal or family crisis. The evidence from practice with couples and from research into divorce shows that the relationship problems which can lead eventually to a decision about separating and divorce can be identified at an early stage in the marriage; that they may be expressed in any one (or more) aspect(s) of a couple's life and that the expression of the disaffection becomes increasingly complicated and for at least one spouse, increasingly unacceptable. At present in our society, the message to couples is that unless someone is distressed or the relationship is in danger of dissolution, existing services are unable or unwilling to respond and that to gain such a response, wife or couple must discover through experience, through trial and error, which agency will accept which 'ticket of entry'. Such resistance to a more flexible, more realistic response, may have been compounded by the debates about specialization, accreditation, professionalization amongst professionals and voluntary workers. These are still not adequately resolved and represent one way of controlling the response to demand and need.

Spouses and couples seek help in relieving problems involving their emotional life, or sexual experiences, their work and leisure, or financial security, their present physical safety or their prospects for the future, their material welfare or their psychological wellbeing. No agency or service, to our knowledge, makes it clear by reputation or by 'word of mouth', far less by open publicity, that it exists in order to respond to the range of problems which can develop during the lifetime of a marriage. If marriage and the maintenance of mutually satisfying marital relationships are as important as our society apparently considers them to be, then we must consider moving towards a more broadly based, generalized marital agency, one which keeps its focus on the marital relationship, but which responds to a recognition that problems within it may vary enormously in their form and severity. Where and how best to locate, fund and support a network of such agencies requires, we think, discussion and consultation between existing professionals and services on the one hand, and the local community on the other. Within such an organization would be required expertise and competence in what is currently called counselling or psychotherapy or casework; in the law pertaining to marriage and family, separation and divorce; in concerns about property, finance and inheritance; in care, custody and access; in marriage, relationships and the life course from young adulthood to old age. If such expertise were to be available within one organization, then there would need to be available a wide range of personnel: counsellors and therapists; solicitors; accountants; experts on rights and entitlements; as well as those who profess a concern for ethics and moral values.

These views do not represent a plea or proposal for the development of some kind of all-embracing, government-funded statutory service. They are an attempt to take seriously the institution called marriage; the realities of long-term heterosexual relationships; the *relative* failure so far, of our organized systems to respond adequately to these realities. We have suggested here that marital problems, throughout the life course of most couples, are not unusual; that if this is so, spouses or couples should be offered the ways and means to explore and hopefully resolve (however partially and temporarily) these problems; and that the dynamic is not one of demand and response, but of a willingness to engage in consultation about how best to promote potential. We think that the current massive demands for the services of the various marriage guidance and marriage advisory services, together with evidence of marital problems from the work of the statutory services, is on the one hand, the tip of the iceberg of need and, on the other, evidence of the desire of a high proportion of married couples to achieve a sufficient degree of mutual satisfaction in their relationship. Our view is that we need to move away from an emphasis on breakdown, or failure, or offence, or crisis, to an organizational and practice approach in which we take seriously the central desire of most couples, at several phases or stages in their relationship, to make of it the best they can.

References

Askham, J. (1984) *Identity and Stability in Marriage*. London: Cambridge University Press.

Backett, K. C. (1982) *Mothers and Fathers*. London: Macmillan.

Barker, P. (1987) *Basic Family Therapy*, 2nd edn. Oxford: Blackwell.

Barrett, M. and McIntosh, M. (1982) *The Anti-Social Family*. London: Verso.

Berger, P. L. and Kellner, H. (1964) Marriage and the construction of reality. *Diogenes*, 1–23.

Berger, P. L. and Luckman T. (1967) *The Social Construction of Reality*. London: Allen Lane.

Bernard, J. (1973) *The Future of Marriage*. New York: Yale University Press.

Bertalanffy, L. Von (1973) *General Systems Theory*. Harmondsworth: Penguin.

Bion, W. (1961) *Experiences in Groups*. London: Tavistock.

Blackie, S. and Clark, D. (1987) Men in marriage counselling. In C. Lewis and M. O'Brien (eds) *Reassessing Fatherhood*. London: Sage.

Blum, A. (1983) Overlapping with general practice. *British Medical Journal*, 286, 21 May 1983, 1619.

BMJ (*British Medical Journal*) (1979) Editorial. 6172, 5 May 1979, 1164.

Bott, E. (1957) *Family and Social Network*. London: Tavistock.

Bowlby, J. (1969 (1973) (1980) *Attachment and Loss*, vols 1–3. London: The Hogarth Press.

—— (1979) *The Making and Breaking of Affectional Bonds*. London: Tavistock.

Brake, M. (1980) *The Sociology of Youth Cultures and Youth Subcultures*. Routledge and Kegan Paul.

Brannen, J. (1988) The study of sensitive subjects. *The Sociological Review*, 36, 3, 552–63.

Brannen, J. and Collard, J. (1982) *Marriages in Trouble*. London: Tavistock.

Bridger, H. (1981) *Consultative Work with Communities and Organisations. Towards a psychodynamic image of man*. The Malcolm Millar Lecture 1980. Aberdeen: Aberdeen University Press.

Brown, G. and Harris, T. (1978) *The Social Origins of Depression*. London: Tavistock.

Buber, M. (1958) *I and Thou* trans. R. G. Smith, 2nd edn. New York: V. Charles Scribners.

Burgoyne, J. (1985) *Cohabitation and Contemporary Family Life*. ESRC (Economic and Social Research Council) end-of-grant report.

—— (1987) Change, gender and the life course. In G. Cohen (ed.) *Social Change and the Life Course*. London: Tavistock.

Burgoyne, J. and Clark, D. (1982) From father to step-father. In L. McKee and M. O'Brien (eds) *The Father Figure*. London: Tavistock.

—— (1984) *Making a Go of It*. London: Routledge and Kegan Paul.

Burgoyne, J., Ormrod, R. and Richards, M. (1987) *Divorce Matters*. Harmondsworth: Penguin.

Busfield, J. (1974) Ideologies and reproduction. in M. P. M. Richards (ed.), *The Integration of a Child into a Social World*. Cambridge: Cambridge University Press.

—— (1987) Parenting and parenthood. In G. Cohen (ed.) *Social Change and the Life Course*. London: Tavistock.

Busfield, J. and Paddon, M. (1977) *Thinking About Children*. London: Cambridge University Press.

Callan, H. and Ardener, S. (eds) (1984) *The Incorporated Wife*. London: Croom Helm.

Chester, R. (1971) Health and marriage breakdown: experience of a sample of divorced women. *British Journal of Preventative and Social Medicine*, 25, 4, 231–5.

—— (1985a) Shaping the future: from marriage movement to service agency. *Marriage Guidance*, Autumn, 5–15.

—— (1985b) Marriage in Britain: an overview of research. In W. Dryden (ed.) *Marital Therapy in Britain*, vol. 1. London: Harper and Row.

Clark, D. (1982) Restarting a family: having children in second marriages. *International Journal of Sociology and Social Policy*, 2, 2, 55–68.

—— (1987) Changing partners: marriage and divorce across the life course. In G. Cohen (ed.) *Social Change and the Life Course*. London: Tavistock.

Clark, D. and Taylor, R. (1988) Partings and reunions: marriage and offshore employment in the British North Sea. In J. Lewis, M. Porter and M. Shrimpton (eds) *Women, Work and Family in the British, Canadian and Norwegian Offshore Oilfields*. London: Macmillan.

Clulow, C. F. (1980) *To Have and to Hold*. Aberdeen: Aberdeen University Press.

—— (1986) *Marital Therapy*. Aberdeen: Aberdeen University Press.

Clulow, C. and Vincent, C. (1987) *In the Child's Best Interests?* London: Tavistock/Sweet and Maxwell.

Coffield, F. (1987) From the celebration to the marginalisation of youth. In G. Cohen (ed.) *Social Change and the Life Course*. London Tavistock.

Cohen, G. (1987) Introduction: the economy, the family and the life course. In G. Cohen (ed.) *Social Change and the Life Course*. London: Tavistock.

Cohen, J. and Halpern, A. (1978) A practice counsellor. *Journal of the Royal College of General Practitioners*, 28, 481–4.

Cooper, D. (1972) *The Death of the Family*. Harmondsworth: Penguin.

Corney, R. H. (1986) Counselling in general practice: the effectiveness of attached social workers. In R. Chester and P. Divall (eds) *Mental Health, Illness and Handicap in Marriage*, Research Report Number 5. Rugby: National Marriage Guidance Council.

Crowe, M. (1985) Marital therapy: a behavioural systems approach – indications for different types of intervention. In W. Dryden (ed.) *Marital Therapy in Britain*, vol. I. London: Harper and Row.

CSO (Central Statistical Office) (1985) *Social Trends*. London: HMSO.

Cunningham-Burley, S. (1987) The experience of grandfatherhood. In C. Lewis and M. O'Brien (eds) *Reassessing Fatherhood*. London: Sage.

Davidoff. L. (1988) Family matters. *History Workshop*, 26, Autumn.

Davidoff, L. and Hall, C. (1987) *Family Fortunes*. London: Hutchinson and University of Chicago Press.

Dennis, N., Henriques, F. M. and Slaughter, C. (1959) *Coal is Our Life*. London: Tavistock.

DHSS (Department of Health and Social Security) (1974) *Report of the Committee on One-Parent Families*, Cmd 5629. London: HMSO.

Dicks, H. V. (1967) *Marital Tensions*. London: Routledge and Kegan Paul.

Dobash, R. P. and Dobash, R. E. (1980) *Violence Against Wives*. Shepton Mallett: Open Books.

Dominian, J. (1969) *Marital Breakdown*. Harmondsworth: Penguin.

—— (1979) *Marital Pathology*. London: Darton Longman and Todd, with BMJ Publications.

Dominian, J. (1980) *Marriage in Britain 1945–80*. London: Study Commission on the Family.

Donzelot, J. (1980) *The Policing of Families*. London: Hutchinson.

Dryden, W. (ed.) (1985) *Marital Therapy in Britain*, 2 vols. London: Harper and Row.

Eichenbaum, L. and Orbach, S. (1984) *What Do Women Want?* New York: Berkeley.

Fairbairn, W. R. D. (1952) *Psychoanalytic Studies of the Personality*. London: Tavistock/Routledge and Kegan Paul.

Finch, J. (1983) *Married to the Job*. London: Allen and Unwin.

Fletcher, R. (1966) *The Family and Marriage in Britain*. Harmondsworth: Penguin.

Forster, N. (1987) Economic and Social Changes in the 1980s: a study of the effects of redundancy on a group of South Yorkshire steel workers and their families. Sheffield City Polytechnic: unpublished PhD thesis.

Foucault, M. (1979) *The History of Sexuality. An Introduction*. London: Allen Lane.

Garfinkel, H. (1967) *Studies in Ethnomethodology*. New York: Prentice Hall.

Gaunt, S. (1985) *The First Interview in Marriage Guidance*, Research Report Number 2. Rugby: National Marriage Guidance Council.

—— (1987) *Reception Interviews in Marriage Guidance*, Research Report Number 6. Rugby: National Marriage Guidance Council.

Gavron, H. (1968) *The Captive Wife*. Harmondsworth: Penguin.

George, V. and Wilding, P. (1972) *Motherless Families*. London: Routledge and Kegan Paul.

Gibson, C. (1974) The association between divorce and social class in England and Wales. *British Journal of Sociology*, 25, 1, 79–93.

Gillis, J. (1985) *For Better, For Worse: British Marriages, 1600 to the Present*. Oxford: Oxford University Press.

Glendon, M. A. (1977) *State, Law and Family*. Amsterdam: North-Holland Publishing.

Goldthorpe, J. et al. (1969) *The Affluent Worker in the Class Structure*. London: Cambridge University Press.

Gorell Barnes, G. (1987) *Making Family Therapy Work: The Application of Research Findings to Practice*. Annual Training Conference, York: Association for Family Therapy.

Green, M. (1984) *Marriage*. London: Fontana.

Greenspan, M. (1983) *A New Approach to Women and Therapy*. New York: McGraw Hill.

Greer, G. (1985) *Sex and Destiny*. London: Picador.

Groot, M. de (1985) *Marriage Guidance Counsellors in the Medical Setting*, Research Report Number 1. Rugby: National Marriage Guidance Council.

Guntrip, H. (1961) *Personality Structure and Human Interaction*. London: The Hogarth Press.

Gurman, A. S. (1978) Contemporary marital therapies: a critique and comparative analysis of psychoanalytic, behavioural and systems theory perspectives. In T. J. Paolino and B. S. McCrady (eds) *Marriage and Marital Therapy*. New York: Brunner/Mazel.

Haldane, J. D. (1982) *A Celebration of Marriage? Scotland 1931–81*. Aberdeen: Aberdeen University Press.

—— (1988) *Marital Therapy: Research, Practice and Organisation*, the Malcolm Miller Lecture, 1987. Aberdeen: Aberdeen University Press.

Haldane, J. D., Alexander, D. A. and Walker, L. G. (1982) *Models for Psychotherapy: a Primer*. Aberdeen: Aberdeen University Press.

Haldane, J. D. and McCluskey, U. (1980a) Working with couples and families: experience of training, consultation and supervision. *Journal of Family Therapy*, 2, 163–79.

—— (1980b) Working with couples and families: a note on some issues for research. Association for Family Therapy *Newsletter*, 26–30.

—— (1981) Working with couples: psychiatrists, clinical psychologists and social workers compared. *Journal of Family Therapy*, 3, 363–88.

—— (1982) Existentialism and family therapy: a neglected perspective. *Journal of Family Therapy*, 4, 117–32.

—— (1988) Therapy with couples and families. In R. E. Kendell and A. Zealley (eds) *Companion to Psychiatric Studies*, 4th edn. Edinburgh: Churchill Livingstone.

Haldane, D., McCluskey, U. and Clark, D. (1986) Does marriage matter? A perspective and model for action. *Journal of Social Work Practice*, May, 31–45.

Haldane, J. D., McCluskey, U. and Peacey, M. (1980) Development of a residential facility for families in Scotland: prospect and retrospect. *International Journal of Family Psychiatry*, 1, 3, 357–71.

Hart, N. (1976) *When Marriage Ends*. London: Tavistock.

Haskey, J. (1982) The proportion of marriages ending in divorce. *Population Trends*, 27, 2–11.

—— (1984) Social class and socio-economic differentials in divorce in England and Wales. *Population Studies*, 38, 419–39.

Hinde, R. A. (1980) Family influences. In M. Rutter (ed.) *Scientific Foundations of Developmental Psychiatry*. London: Heinemann.

Hipgrave, T. (1982) Lone fatherhood: a problematic status. In M. O'Brien and L. McKee (eds) *The Father Figure*. London: Tavistock.

HMSO (Her Majesty's Stationery Office) (1948) *Report of the Departmental Committee on Grants for the Development of Marriage Guidance*, Cmd 7566.

Hollowell, P. G. (1968) *The Lorry Driver*. London: Routledge and Kegan Paul.

Hooper, D. (1985) Marital therapy: an overview of research. In W. Dryden (ed.) *Marital Therapy in Britain*, vol. 2. London: Harper and Row.

Horstman, A. (1985) *Victorian Divorce*. London: Croom Helm.

Hunt, P. (1985) *Clients' Responses to Marriage Counselling*, Research Report Number 3. Rugby: National Marriage Guidance Council.

Ineichen, B. (1977) Youthful marriage: the vortex of disadvantage. In R. Chester and J. Peel (eds) *Equalities and Inequalities in Family Life*. London: Academic Press.

James, A. L. and Wilson, K. (1986) *Couples, Conflict and Change*. London: Tavistock.

Kaslow, K. W. (1977) Training of marital and family therapists. In K. W. Kaslow and associates *Supervision, Consultation and Staff Training in the Helping Professions*. London: Jossey-Bass.

Keithley, J. (1982) Marriage counselling – general practice: an assessment of the work of marriage guidance counsellors in a general practice. University of Durham: unpublished PhD thesis.

Kiernan, K. (1985) The departure of children: the timing of leaving home over the life cycles of parents and children. *Centre for Population Studies Research Paper* 85, 3. University of London.

La Fontaine, J. (1985) Anthropological perspectives on the family and social change. *The Quarterly Journal of Social Affairs*, 1, 1, 29–56.

Laing, R. D. (1971) *The Politics of the Family*. London: Tavistock.

Lasch, C. (1977) *Haven in Heartless World*. New York: Basic Books.

Lawson, A. (1988) *Adultery*. New York: Basic Books.

Leach, E. (1967) *A Runaway World?* London: British Broadcasting Corporation.

Lenn, M. H. (1980) *The out-posted volunteer. A study of the relationship between Marriage Guidance Councils and the statutory agencies*. University of Dundee: unpublished.

Lewis, C. (1986) *Becoming a Father*. Milton Keynes: Open University Press.

Lewis, C. and O'Brien, M. (eds) (1987) *Reassessing Fatherhood*. London: Sage.

Lewis, J. (1984) *Women in England 1870–1950*. Sussex: Wheatsheaf.

Lynch, J. J. (1977) *The Broken Heart*. New York: Basic Books.

Macfarlane, A. (1987) *Marriage and Love in England: Modes of Reproduction 1300–1840*. Oxford: Basil Blackwell.

Macintyre, S. (1976) Who wants babies? The social construction of 'instincts'. In D. L. Barker and S. Allen (eds) *Sexual Divisions and Society*. London: Tavistock.

—— (1985) *Marriage is good for your health; or is it?* Lecture given to the Royal Philosophical Society of Glasgow, 11 December 1985.

Mackay, D. (1985) Marital therapy: the behavioural approach. In W. Dryden (ed.) *Marital Therapy in Britain*, vol. 1. London: Harper and Row.

—— (1985) Approaches to marital therapy: comparative analyses. A behavioural therapist's point of view, In W. Dryden (ed.) *Marital Therapy in Britain*, vol. 1. London: Harper and Row.

Macquarrie, J. (1973) *Existentialism*. Harmondsworth: Penguin.

McRobbie, A. (1978) Working class girls and the culture of femininity. In Women's Studies Group (eds) *Women Take Issue*. London: Hutchinson.

Mansfield, P. (1985) *Young People and Marriage*, Occasional Paper Number 1. Edinburgh: Scottish Marriage Guidance Council.

Mansfield, P. and Collard, J. (1988) *The Beginning of the Rest of Your Life?* London: Macmillan.

Marriage Matters (1979) Report of the Working Party on Marriage Guidance. London: HMSO.

Marris, P. (1958) *Widows and Their Families*. London: Routledge and Kegan Paul.

Marsden, D. (1969) *Mothers Alone*. London: Allen Lane.

Martin, J. and Roberts, C. (1984) *Women and Employment: A Lifetime Perspective*. London: HMSO.

Mason, J. (1987) A bed of roses? Women, marriage and inequality in later life. In P. Allatt, T. Keil, A. Bryman and B. Bytheway (eds) *Women and the Life Cycle*. London: Macmillan.

Masters, W. and Johnson, V. (1966) *Human Sexual Response*. London: Churchill.

Matheson, S. M. G. and Gentleman, H. (1986) *The Scottish Family Conciliation Service (Lothian)*. Edinburgh: Scottish Office Central Research Unit.

Mattinson, J. (1988) *Love, Work and Marriage*. London: Duckworth.

Mattinson, J. and Sinclair, I. (1979) *Mate and Stalemate*. Oxford: Basil Blackwell.

Miller, E. J. (ed.) (1976) *Task and Organisation*. London: John Wiley.

Mintz, S. (1983) *A Prison of Expectations: The Family in Victorian Culture*. New York: New York University Press.

Morgan D. H. J. (1982) *Berger and Kellner's construction of the family*. University of Manchester, Department of Sociology: Occasional Paper Number 7.

—— (1985) *The Family, Politics and Social Theory*. London: Routledge and Kegan Paul.

Morrice, J. K. W. (1981) Couple therapy in a therapeutic community setting. *Journal of Family Therapy*, 3, 353–61.

Morris, L. (1985) Redundancy and patterns of household finance. *Sociological Review*, 32, 492–523.

Nissel, M. (1987) Social change and the family cycle. In G. Cohen (ed.) *Social Change and the Life Course*. London: Tavistock.

NMGC (1986) *Seizing the Challenge of Change*, Report prepared by Coopers and Lybrand Associates. Rugby: National Marriage Guidance Council.

Oakley, A. (1974) *The Sociology of Housework*. Oxford: Martin Robertson.

—— (1981) Interviewing women: a contradiction in terms. In C. Bell and H. Roberts (eds) *Social Researching*. London: Routledge and Kegan Paul.

O'Brien, M. and McKee, L. (eds) (1982) *The Father Figure*. London: Tavistock.

OPCS (Office of Population Censuses and Surveys) (1984) *Marriage and Divorce*, OPCS Monitor FM2 84/2. London: OPCS.

Pahl, J. (ed.) (1985) *Private Violence and Public Policy*. London: Routledge and Kegan Paul.

Paolino, T. J. and McCrady, B. S. (eds) (1978) *Marriage and Marital Therapy*. New York: Brunner/Mazel.

Parkinson, L. (1986) *Conciliation in Separation and Divorce*. London: Croom Helm.

Parsons, T. and Bales, R. F. (1956) *Family Socialisation and Interaction Process*. London: Routledge and Kegan Paul.

Rapoport, R. and Rapoport, R. N. (1976) *Dual Career Families Re-examined*. Oxford: Martin Robertson.

Rapoport, R., Rapoport, R. N. and Strelitz, Z. (1977) *Fathers, Mothers and Others*. London: Routledge and Kegan Paul.

Report of the Conciliation Project Unit (1989). University of Newcastle-upon-Tyne, forthcoming.

Richards, M. P. M. (1982) The changing role of men. In S. Saunders (ed.) *Change in Marriage*. Rugby: National Marriage Guidance Council.

Richman, J. (1982) Men's experience of pregnancy and childbirth. In M. O'Brien and L. McKee (eds) *The Father Figure*. London: Tavistock.

Ricoeur, P. (1976) *Interpretation Theory*. Fort Worth: Texas Christian University Press.

Rimmer, L. (1981) *Families in Focus*. London: Study Commission on the Family.

Rogers, C. (1961) *On Becoming a Person*. London: Constable.

Rutter, M. (1972) *Maternal Deprivation Reassessed*. Harmondsworth: Penguin.

Rycroft, C. (1972) *A Critical Dictionary of Psychoanalysis*. Harmondsworth: Penguin.

Sanders, D. (1983) *The Woman Report on Men*. London: Sphere.

—— (1985) *The Woman Book of Love and Sex*. London: Michael Joseph.

Sarsby, J. (1983) *Romantic Love and Society*. Harmondsworth: Penguin.

Schutz, A. (1964) *The Collected Papers*, 2 vols. The Hague: Nijhoff.

Semeonoff, B. (1985) Changes and trends in counsellor selection. *News-sheet*, May. Edinburgh: Scottish Marriage Guidance Council.

Sennett, R. (1974) *The Fall of Public Man*. London: Cambridge University Press.

Skynner, R. (1976) *One Flesh: Separate Persons*. London: Constable.

—— (1980) Recent developments in marital therapy. *Journal of Family Therapy*, 2, 271–96.

Smart, C. (1984) *The Ties that Bind*. London: Routledge and Kegan Paul.

SMGC (1986) *A Five Year Plan 1985–90*. Edinburgh, Scottish Marriage Guidance Council.

Smith M. and Simms, C. (1982) Young fathers: attitudes to marriage and family life. In M. O'Brien and L. McKee (eds) *The Father Figure*. London: Tavistock.

Study Commission on the Family (1983) *Families in the Future*. London: Study Commission on the Family.

The Times (1988) Mind over marriage. 6 February 1988.

Thornes, B. and Collard, J. (1979) *Who Divorces?* London: Routledge and Kegan Paul.

Townsend, P. (1957) *The Family Life of Old People*. London: Routledge and Kegan Paul.

Toynbee, P. (1983) The counsellor in the doctor's chair. *The Guardian*, 25 July 1983.

Treacher, A. (1985) Working with marital partners: systems approaches. In W. Dryden (ed.) *Marital Therapy in Britain*, vol. 1. London: Harper and Row.

Trumbach, R. (1978) *The Rise of the Egalitarian Family*. New York: Academic Press.

Tunstall, J. (1962) *The Fishermen*. London: McGibbon and Kee.

Tyndall, N. (1982) Conciliation: an overview. *Marriage Guidance*, 20, 3, 113–18.

Visher, E. B. and Visher, J. S. (1979) *Stepfamilies*. New York: Brunner/Mazel.

Voysey, M. (1975) *A Constant Burden*. London: Routledge and Kegan Paul.

Walker, L. G. (1982) The behavioural model. In J. D. Haldane, D. A. Alexander and L. G. Walker *Models for Psychotherapy: a Primer*. Aberdeen: Aberdeen University Press.

Walrond-Skinner, S. (1979) Education or training for family therapy? A reconstruction. In S. Walrond-Skinner (ed.) *Family and Marital Psychotherapy*. London: Routledge and Kegan Paul.

Watkins, J. M. (1983) Marriage counselling in our practice. *British Medical Journal*, 287, 17 September 1983, 808.

Watney, S. (1987) *Policing Desire*. London: Comedia.

Weeks, J. (1981) *Sex, Politics and Society*, London: Longman.

Willis, P. (1977) *Learning to Labour*. London: Saxon House.

—— (1984) Youth employment 1: a new social state. *New Society*, April, 475–77.

Winnicott, D. W. (1958) *Collected Papers*. London: Tavistock.

—— (1965a) *The Maturational Processes and the Facilitating Environment*. London: The Hogarth Press.

—— (1965b) *The Family and Individual Development*. London: Tavistock.

—— (1971) *Playing and Reality*. London: Tavistock.

Wright Mills, C. (1959) *The Sociological Imagination*. London: Oxford University Press.

Young, M. and Willmott, P. (1957) *Family and Kinship in East London*. London: Routledge and Kegan Paul.

—— (1973) *The Symmetrical Family*. Harmondsworth: Penguin.

Subject Index